# Melodic Banjo

### by Tony Trischka

A complete instruction guide to the "Keith style" banjo technique.

To access audio visit:
www.halleonard.com/mylibrary

Enter Code
6127-5233-8826-9358

Visit Hal Leonard Online at
www.halleonard.com

Contact Us:
**Hal Leonard**
7777 West Bluemound Road
Milwaukee, WI 53213
Email: info@halleonard.com

In Europe contact:
**Hal Leonard Europe Limited**
42 Wigmore Street
Marylebone, London, W1U 2RN
Email: info@halleonardeurope.com

In Australia contact:
**Hal Leonard Australia Pty. Ltd.**
4 Lentara Court
Cheltenham, Victoria, 3192 Australia
Email: info@halleonard.com.au

**Dedication**
*This book is dedicated to Earl Scruggs, Bill Keith, and Bobby Thompson-without whom this book wouldn't exist; my family-John, Coryl, Dale, and Sugar Trischka-for everything; Wendy Heitzman-for love, patience, and the writing of tablature at late hours; Peter Wernick-who has helped me in more ways than I can mention; Gail Kramer-for friendship and good typing; Bela Fleck-for enthusiasm and transcribing.*

**Acknowledgements**
Special thanks to my friends at Oak Publications: Jason Shulman, Arthur Steinman, Debbie Schwartz, Iris Weinstein, Mark Stein, Carol Zimmerman, and Gordon Williams, and to everyone else who helped make this book possible.

**Photo Credits:**
*courtesy of* The Country Music Foundation Library and Media Center 16
Bluegrass Unlimited 21
John Lee 25
Great Lakes Banjo Company 28
John Delgatto/Bluegrass Unlimited 37
Grease Brothers/Jim McGuire 43
David Gahr 44
David Gahr 46
Windchime Music 49
Courtesy of Millie Clements 60
Bluegrass Unlimited 61
George Pickow 63
David Gahr 65
Julie Snow 71
Bluegrass Unlimited 72
Bluegrass Unlimited 73
John Lee 77
John Lee 82
Grease Brothers/Jim McGuire 86
Bluegrass Unlimited 87
Tom Hosmer 90
Bluegrass Unlimited 92
Jack Rummel/Pickin' Magazine 94
Don Kissil/Pickin' Magazine 95
Grease Brothers/Jim McGuire 100
Harold E. Sturm 105
Iris Weinstein 106
Artie Rose 113
Grease Brothers/Jim McGuire 125

Book design by Iris Weinstein
All technical photos by Mark Stein

Oak Publications has conducted an exhaustive search to locate the composers, publishers, or copyright owners of the compositions in this book. However, in the event that we have inadvertently published a previously copyrighted composition without proper acknowledgement, we advise the copyright owner to contact us so that we may give appropriate credit in future editions.

Copyright © 1976 by Oak Publications,
A Division of Music Sales Corporation, New York, NY

All rights reserved. No part of this book may be reproduced in any form or by any electronic or mechanical means including information storage and retrieval systems, without permission in writing from the publisher except by a reviewer who may quote brief passages in review.

International Standard Book Number: 978.0.8256.0171.2
Library of Congress Catalog Card Number: 75-16978

# Contents

Introduction 5

Getting Started 7
   Tuning 7
   Holding the Banjo 8

Basic Chord Positions 9
   Inversions 12
   The Capo 13

Reading Tablature 14
   Repeat Sign 15
   Triplets 15

Scruggs Style 16
   Fingerpicks 16
   Right Hand Position 17
   Basic Rolls 17
   Basic Licks 18
   *Cripple Creek* 21
   *Old Joe Clark* 22
   Choking 23
   Harmonics 23

Reno Style 25

The Melodic Style 26

Bill Keith 28
   *Blackberry Blossom* 34
   *Little Sadie* 35
   *Arkansas Traveler* 36
   *New Camptown Races* 37
   *Opus 57 In G Minor* 40
   Interview with Bill Keith 42

Melodic Blues Runs 47

Bobby Thompson 49
   *Katy Hill* 53
   *Are You Missing Me* 54
   *Devil Dance* and *Foxfire* 55
   Interview with Bobby Thompson 59

Chromatic Runs 62

Eric Weissberg and Marshall Brickman 63
   *Devil's Dream* 66
   *Eighth Of January* 67
   *Fire On The Mountain* 68
   *Shuckin' The Corn* 69
   Interview with Eric Weissberg 70

Second Generation Melodic Players 72
   Ben Eldridge 72
   *Muddy Water* 75
   *Gardens And Memories* 75
   *Cross Country* 76
   Jack Hicks 77
   *Indian Blood* 79
   *Grey Eagle* 80
   Carl Jackson 82
   *Bill Cheatham* 84
   *Done Gone* 85
   Courtney Johnson 86
   *Cold Sailor* 88
   *Lonesome Fiddle Blues* 89
   Vic Jordan 90
   *Turkey In The Straw* 92
   *Jordan's Hornpipe* 93
   Alan Munde 94
   *Dusty Miller* 97
   *Lonesome Blues* 98

Working Up Songs On Your Own 99

**Melodic Backup** 101

**Improvising Melodically** 102

**Fiddle Tune Finale** 106
   *Paddy On The Turnpike* 107
   *John Hardy* 108
   *June Apple* 109
   *Rickett's Hornpipe* 110
   *Soldier's Joy* 111
   *Red Haired Boy* 112
   *Sally Goodin* 113
   *Fisher's Hornpipe* 114
   *Sleepy Hollow Real* 115
   *Twelve Weeks At Sea* 116

**Appendices** 117

   Music Theory 117

   A Few Notes on Setting Up
   Your Banjo to Play Bluegrass
   by Tom Hosmer 119

   Banjo Playing:
   Reno-Thompson-Scruggs-Keith
   Style and Beyond
   by Steve Arkin 122

**Discography** 126

**Song Index** 127

# Introduction

As you pick up this book, you may be wondering exactly what melodic style banjo is. Perhaps you already know it by one of its aliases—the *chromatic*, *Keith*, or *fiddle tune* style. No matter what you call it, it stands as *the* most important advance in bluegrass banjo technique since Scruggs style.

Earl Scruggs gave us drive, syncopation, and the smooth, three-finger right hand roll. What he didn't provide for us, though, was a way to play scales or the long, flowing melody lines that grow out of them. This breakthrough was accomplished by Bobby Thompson and Bill Keith, who developed the melodic style in the late 1950s and early 1960s. With this new style, it became possible for a banjo player to pick fiddle tunes note-for-note as the fiddler would. In addition, an entirely new repertoire of exciting licks and runs grew up; and suddenly, there was something to play besides Scruggs style.

This book will teach you the melodic approach as interpreted by Bill Keith, Bobby Thompson and the other men who contributed to its popularity. By means of interviews, quotes, musical examples and songs, you'll gain a thorough understanding of what's involved in the style, technically and historically. If you're just beginning to play the banjo, you'll find a short section on Scruggs style which will give you the basics you'll need to move comfortably through the rest of the book. But most important, you'll learn how to improvise melodically which, in turn, will allow you to bring your own personality into your playing. Remember, the melodic style should serve as a tool for developing your creativity rather than as an end in itself.

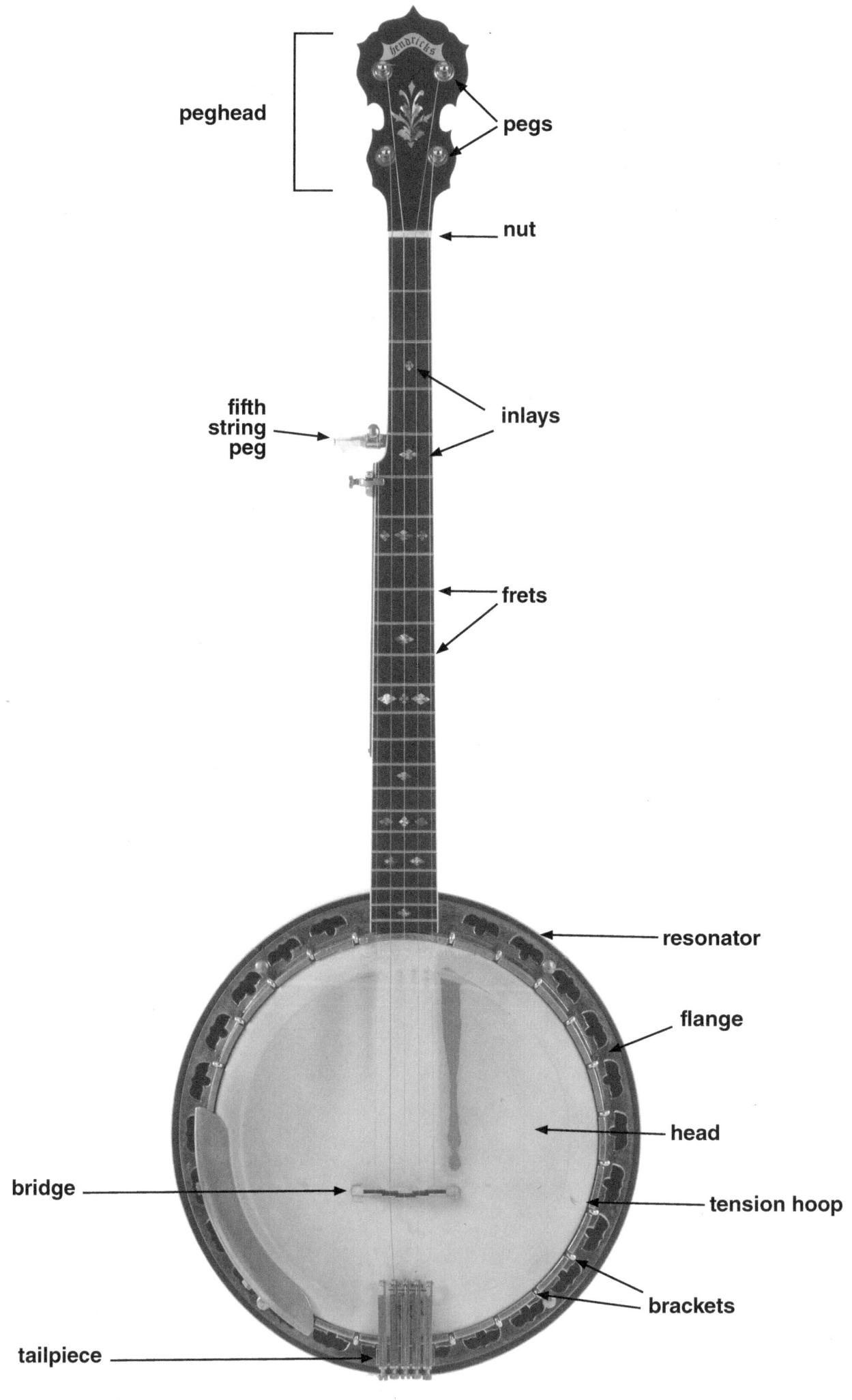

# Getting Started

tuning

Before you begin playing music you'll want to make sure your banjo's in tune. The easiest way to do this is by getting a note or notes from another instrument which is already in tune. If you have access to a piano, simply tune the strings of the banjo to the corresponding notes on the keyboard.

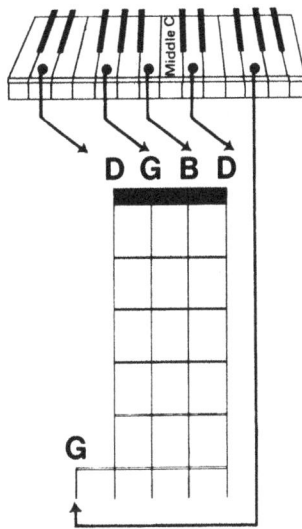

When you hear these notes, determine whether the corresponding banjo notes are flat (below) or sharp (above) in relationship to the piano. Keep hitting the banjo string while you're turning the tuning peg so that you can keep track of where you are. If you have trouble hearing when the note is in tune, don't worry. Your *ear* will improve with practice.

You can also have someone play a single note (preferably a G, D or B note) on a guitar or any other instrument and tune to that. Once one string is in tune, you can tune the rest of the strings to it by this method:

Match the fifth fret of the fourth string with the open third string (G).
Match the fourth fret of the third string with the open second string (B).
Match the third fret of the second string with the open first string (D).
Match the fifth fret of the first string with the open fifth string (G).

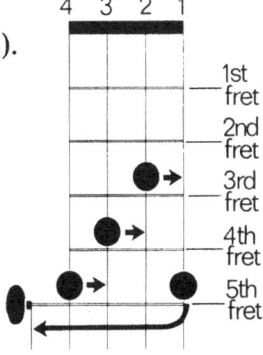

If you can't find another instrument you can always tune to a record. Pick a song that's in the key of G such as Marshall Brickman's version of "Shuckin' the Corn," get your G string in tune with it, and work from there.

Another alternative is to buy a tuning fork. This is more accurate and portable and can be bought in almost any music store. When a tuning fork is struck, it produces an A440 (an A note vibrating at 440 cycles per second). This is the note that determines *concert* or *standard* pitch for all other instruments.

To get in tune by this method, hold the tuning fork by its handle and strike one prong against your knee. Then, while it's still vibrating, place the handle on top of the bridge of the banjo and you'll hear the A note being amplified by the vibrations of the bridge on the head.

Since the standard bluegrass tuning for banjo has no open A strings, you'll have to press down the third string at the second fret to get the A in tune. At this point you can tune the rest of the strings to the third string.

Keep in mind, though, that you don't always have to be exactly in tune with concert pitch. Just be sure you're in tune with yourself and the people with whom you're playing.

holding the banjo

When you're playing by yourself you'll usually be sitting down, in which case you can rest the banjo in your lap or on your knee—whichever feels more comfortable. However, when you play with other people in a bluegrass setting, you'll probably be standing, which means that you'll want to use a strap. The strap can be attached to the brackets on the banjo and should be adjusted so that the instrument is at a comfortable height.

The banjo neck should be held between the thumb and the rest of the fingers of the left hand. Hold it tightly enough so that the banjo won't fall on the floor, but loosely enough so that there's no strain in your hand. The fingers of your left hand should be poised directly above the strings so that you're able to move quickly between positions.

# Basic Chord Positions

Since a lot of bluegrass is played out of the G position on the banjo, you should learn the three most commonly used chords in the key of G: G, C and D.

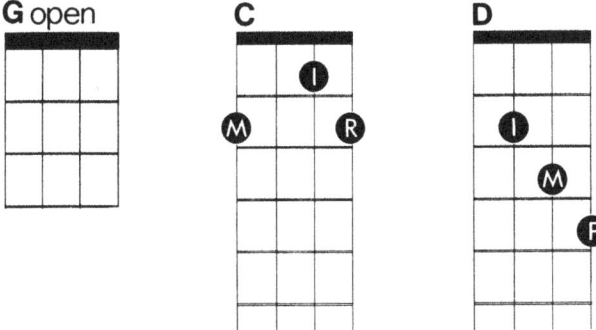

These three chords can also be called I, IV and V chords, respectively. These numbers refer to the chords which are built around the first, fourth and fifth notes of any scale in which you're playing. (See Appendix 1 for more details.) In the key of C, the I, IV and V chords are C, F and $G^7$:

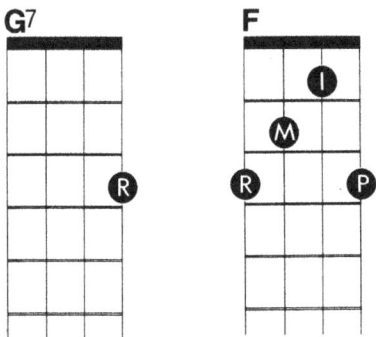

Most bluegrass songs, and in fact most popular songs in general, are based on the I, IV and V chord progression. Musicians will refer to chords by these numbers because in many cases, it's easier to do this than to call them by their letter names.

This next diagram, taken from Peter Wernick's book, *Bluegrass Banjo* (Oak Publications), lists all of the main chords in the seven major keys, including the II, VI and VII chords:

|      | I | IV | V  | II | VI | VII |
|------|---|----|----|----|----|-----|
|   A  | A | D  | E  | B  | F# | G   |
|   B  | B | E  | F# | C# | G# | A   |
|   C  | C | F  | G  | D  | A  | B♭  |
| Keys D | D | G  | A  | E  | B  | C   |
|   E  | E | A  | B  | F# | C# | D   |
|   F  | F | B♭ | C  | G  | D  | E♭  |
|   G  | G | C  | D  | A  | E  | F   |

If you're playing a song in the key of G and you want to move it to the key of C to make it easier for you to sing or play, just look at the chart to see what the corresponding I, IV and V chords are in the new key. This moving from one key to another is called *transposing*. Here are a few more chords that will help you transpose into more keys:

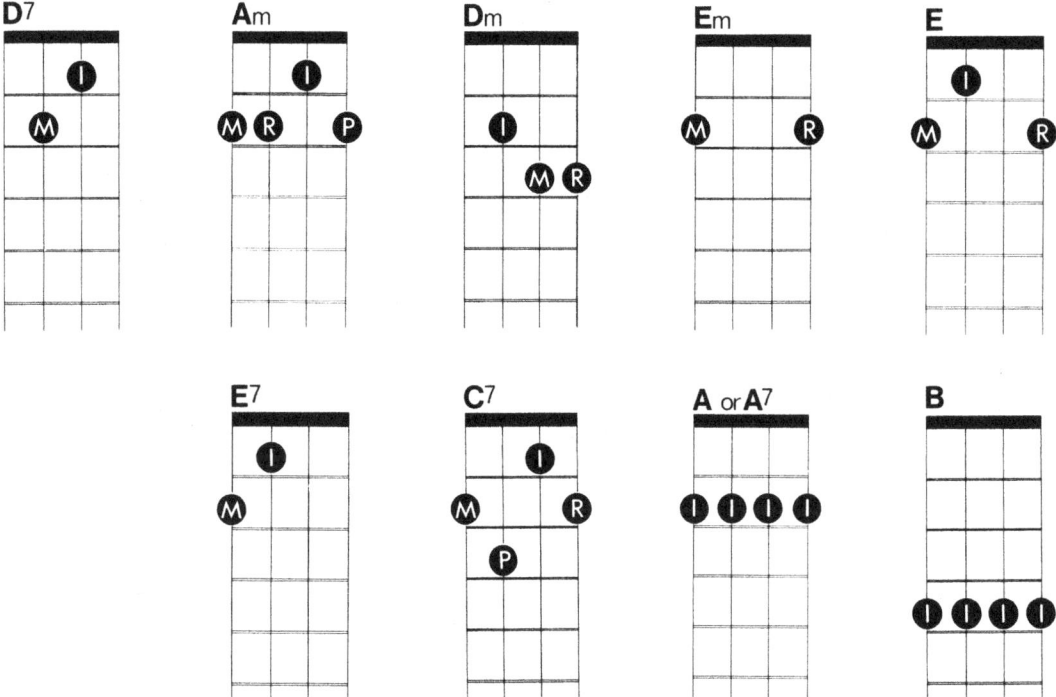

10

Now that you know them, strum through these next few well-known songs to practice changing chords smoothly. Since I'm using the I, IV and V designations, it will be up to you to choose the specific key for each song. Try to get comfortable with the idea of transposing. (The heavy lines indicate downbeats, the light ones, offbeats.)

**Red River Valley**

```
            I
From this valley they say you are going
 /   / /   / /   / /   /
     I                  V
We will miss your bright eyes and sweet smile;
 /   / /   / /        / /
     I              IV
For they say you are taking the sunshine
 /    / /   / /   / /
     V              I
That has brightened our path for awhile.
 /      /   /   / /   /
```
Come and sit by my side if you love me
Do not hasten to bid me adieu;
But remember the Red River Valley
And the cowboy who loved you so true.

**Amazing Grace**

```
 I              IV      I
Amazing Grace, how sweet the sound
/ / /   /   /   /   /   /
 I              V
That saved a wretch like me.
/   / /   /   /   /
 I              IV      I
I once was lost but now I'm found
/ / /   /   /   /   /
 I      V       I
Was blind but now I see.
/   /   / /   /   /
```

If you find that you're getting *string buzz*, it may mean that your fingers are too far away from the frets. They should be close to the frets, but not on top of them.

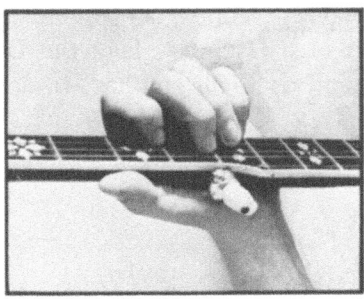

If you're still having trouble changing chords, play the songs more slowly. The important thing is to keep a steady rhythm and play the chords cleanly.

inversions

An *inversion* is simply another way of fingering the same chord at a different part of the fingerboard. For instance, this is a G chord,

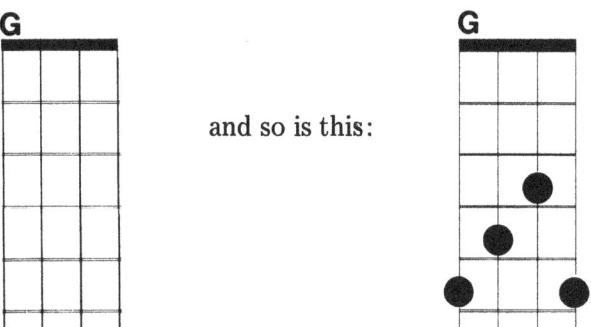

and so is this:

Notice that the second inversion is the same as an F chord moved up two frets. The best way to understand this is by becoming familiar with the notes of an octave on a piano keyboard (again, see Appendix 1 for more details).

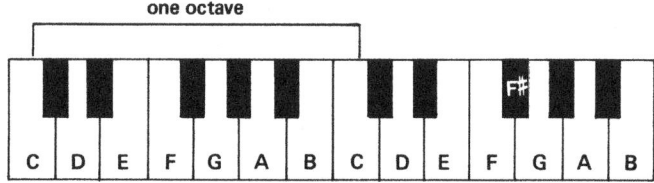

Every time you go from one piano key to the very next one, black or white, or from one banjo fret to the next consecutive one, you're moving one half step. This is known as *moving chromatically*. Thus, there are two half steps between F and G—from F to F♯ and from F♯ to G. So if you know an F chord and you want to play a G chord, simply move the position up two frets. To find the next highest inversion of a G chord, take the D chord and you'll find that there are five half steps between it and G. So all you have to do is move your D position up five frets:

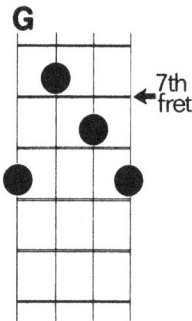

Once you've gotten the hang of this system, you'll be able to find the different inversions for any chord. Keep referring to the keyboard until it becomes second nature to you.

the capo

The capo is a device which clamps onto the neck of your instrument and helps you to play in different keys without changing basic left hand positions. For bluegrass music you'll usually want to play out of a G, C or D position. Suppose, though, that your band is playing in the key of B. Normally, this would give you some trouble. But if you have a capo, you can put it on the fourth fret (B is four half steps above G) and still play out of the open G position.

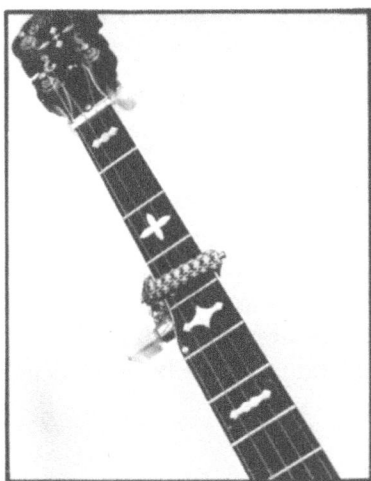

Basically, the capo makes it very easy for you to transpose from one key to another. This is where the I, IV and V terminology comes in handy. Suppose that the musicians you're playing with are in the key of B. Since you'll be capoed at the fourth fret on the banjo, you'll probably still be thinking in terms of G, C and D. However, anyone not using a capo, such as a fiddler or mandolinist, will be looking at it in terms of B, E and F♯. To reach a common understanding, all parties involved can refer to the I, IV and V chords. (See Appendix 2 for information about fifth string capos.)

# Reading Tablature

The music in this book will be written out in *tablature*. Tablature is a simple method of reading and writing music which applies specifically to the instrument for which it is written. You don't have to read music to understand it.

In our case, we'll be using a five line *staff*, with each line representing a string on the banjo:

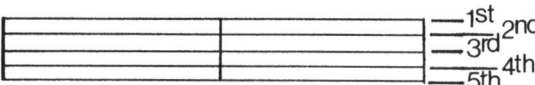

The vertical lines in the above example divide the staff into equal sections called measures. The length of the measure in a particular song is determined by the *time signature*. For instance, in bluegrass music—and in this book—most of the tunes are in 2/4 time. The 2 refers to the number of beats in each measure, and the 4 to the value of the beat. Thus in 2/4 time there are *two quarter* notes per measure.

This time signature can also be broken down to four eighth notes,

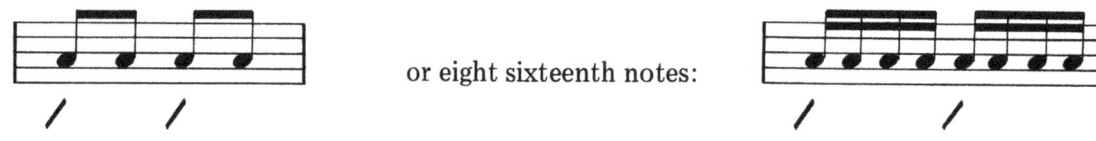

or eight sixteenth notes:

In this book we'll generally be working with eight sixteenth notes per measure.

However, in tablature, numbers rather than notes are written on the lines of the staff to indicate what fret of which string is to be fingered by the left hand. For instance, to play the third fret of the second string you would find this notation:

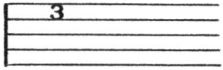

In the case of an open string, an "O" is used. An "X" on the middle line refers to a *rest* (or space where no note is played) equal in value to the other notes in the measure.

Underneath each number is an indication as to how the right hand will pick that note:

    T = thumb
    1 = index finger
    2 = middle finger

Here's an example:

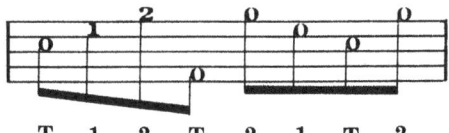

T  1  2  T  2  1  T  2

repeat sign

The signs 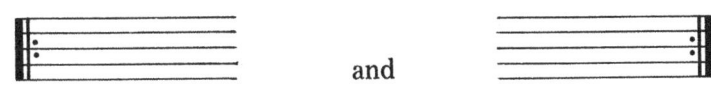 and

mean that you should repeat the section enclosed by them. In most cases in this book, you'll be repeating entire verses or choruses. If there is no

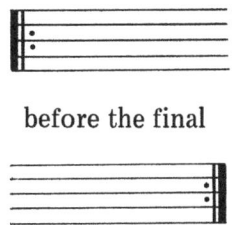

before the final

you should go back to the beginning of the section. When the section to be repeated has two separate endings, it is indicated like this:

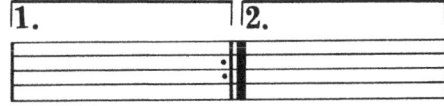

This means that you should play through the entire section once, using the first ending; then go back to the beginning and play it through again, this time skipping the first ending and playing the second one.

triplets

A triplet is a group of three notes which is performed in the same length of time as two. You can use it most effectively to give a little extra push to the beginning or end of a song. Here's how a triplet looks in tablature:

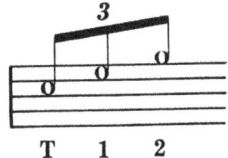

T  1  2

Listen to "Rickett's Hornpipe" on the insert record because it contains a good number of triplets.

# Scruggs Style

The most influential banjo player in the history of bluegrass music has undoubtedly been Earl Scruggs. He first gained recognition in 1945 while playing with Bill Monroe's *Bluegrass Boys* on the Grand Ole Opry stage. Back then people referred to his three finger style as "that fancy banjo playin'." It emphasized the basic melody notes of a song and filled in the spaces between them with ornamental background notes. This resulted in a fast flowing sound that excited audiences all around the South.

L to R: Birch Monroe, Chubby Wise, Bill Monroe, Lester Flatt and Earl Scruggs

In recent years, such hits as "The Theme from Deliverance", "The Ballad of Jed Clampett" and "Foggy Mountain Breakdown" have given the Scruggs sound international popularity. Since Scruggs style serves as a foundation for the melodic style, you should go over the techniques outlined in this chapter before moving on to the rest of the book.

fingerpicks

Although at first you'll probably be playing by yourself, the time will come when you'll want to make music with others. To do this you should be able to get as much sound as you need out of your banjo, especially if you want to play with a full band. Enter the fingerpick. You should wear two of them (National brand works fine) on the index and middle fingers of your right hand, plus a thumbpick for the thumb. In the beginning you may find the metallic sound of the picks hitting the strings so distracting you'll want to forget the whole thing. But don't get discouraged. Stick with the picks and in a short time you'll forget they're even there.

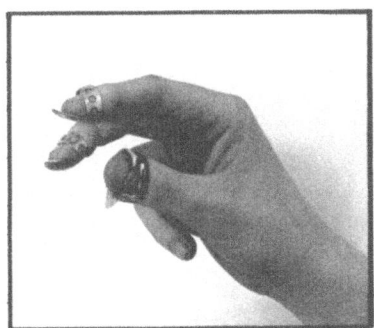

right hand position

To start with, you'll be using the thumb, index finger and middle finger of the right hand to pick. Your ring finger and pinky should be placed on the head of the banjo, about half an inch in front of the bridge, for support. However, when playing backup banjo you'll sometimes want to move your hand farther away from the bridge to get a softer sound. Also you should be sure that your hand is arched slightly from the wrist. This will give you a cleaner, more direct attack on the strings.

basic rolls

A *roll* refers to the order in which the three fingers of the right hand pick the strings. There are three basic rolls that are used in Scruggs style.

First is the forward roll, which is simply the thumb, index and middle fingers picking the strings in that order:

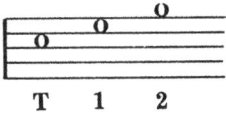

The forward roll is important because it provides a lot of the driving sound associated with bluegrass. (Ralph Stanley uses it a lot in his playing.)

Next is the backward roll, which is the opposite of the forward roll:

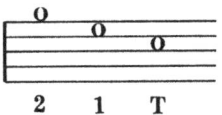

Finally, there is what I call the T 1 T 2 roll:

Some people refer to this roll as three finger double-thumbing because you alternate the thumb with the index and middle fingers.

Here's a simple version of "Little Maggie" incorporating these rolls:

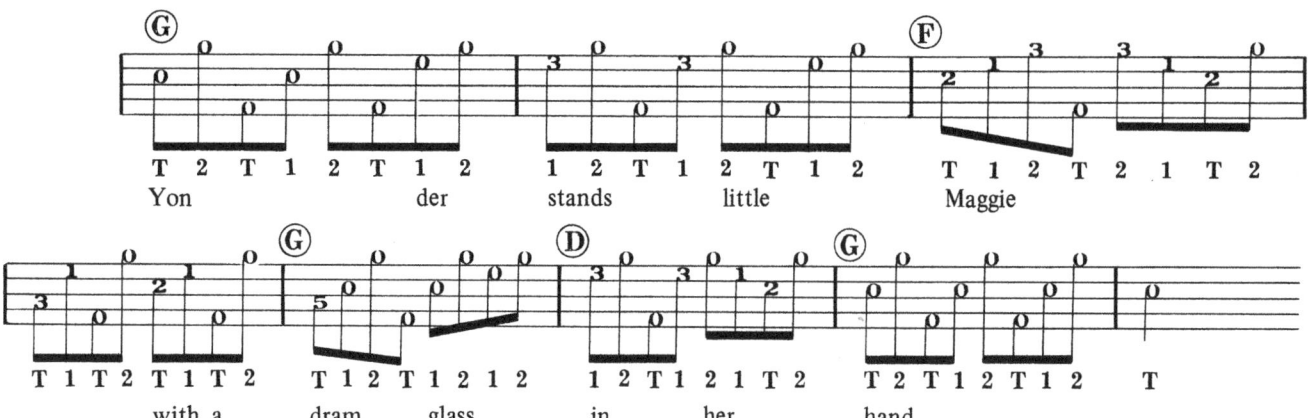

Of course these aren't the only rolls to be played on the banjo, but they show up over and over again in standard Scruggs style.

basic licks

With these next four licks, we're going to get to the roots of bluegrass. These are standard Scruggs licks that you hear again and again in bluegrass songs.

The first three use the T 1 T 2 roll, so you shouldn't have any trouble with the right hand. Each of these licks features a different left hand technique essential to achieving the Scruggs sound.

The first is the *slide*, which involves picking a fretted string and then sliding the fretting finger of your left hand to a different fret.

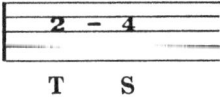

Now try this lick:

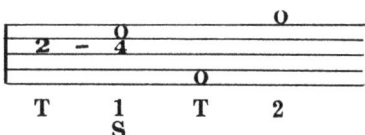

Here, the middle finger of the left hand slides from the second to the fourth fret of the third string, emphasizing the first note of the slide. As you reach the fourth fret at the end of the slide, you should pick the second string.

Next is the *pull-off*, which is simply pulling or pushing a finger of the left hand off a string. You can pull off either to a fretted note,

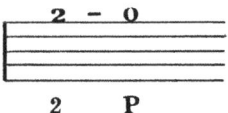

or to an open one:

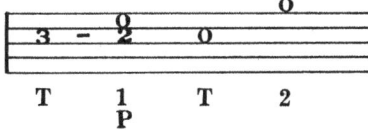

This isn't a difficult technique but it does take a certain amount of finesse to get it to sound right. You shouldn't just lift your finger off the string when you're pulling off. You should use more of a quick upward or downward motion so that you're actually picking the string with your left hand. (Thus, in many cases, the finger that is pulling off will brush lightly against the adjacent string as you complete the pull-off.) Here's a common lick using this technique:

This lick should be played by pulling off in an upward direction (toward the fifth string) with the middle finger of the left hand while fretting the second fret with your index finger.

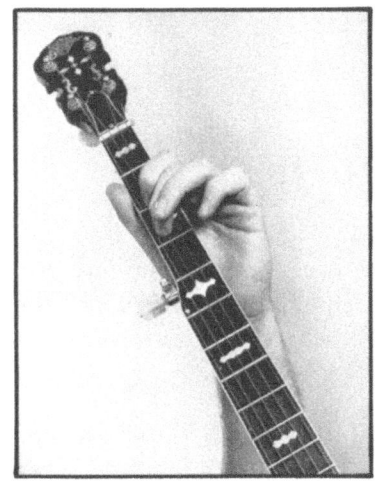

Now let's consider the direction of other pull-offs. If the pull-off covers two frets or more, then you'll usually want to pull down on the string. If the distance covered is only one fret, the direction of your stroke can vary. In the case of the first string, the pull-off will be a downward movement. For the second, third and fourth strings, the pull-off is generally upward. J. D. Crowe is just about the best in the business when it comes to the snappy pull-off. So if you can get yours to sound like his, you'll be in good shape.

The last of these three techniques is the *hammer-on* which refers to picking an open or fretted string with the right hand, then hammering on to a higher note with a finger of the left hand.

Try this—hit the open fourth string with your right thumb, then quickly fret the string at the second fret with your left middle finger.

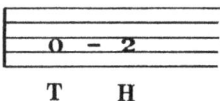

Keep playing this until you can hear the open and fretted note distinctly. Here's a T 1 T 2 lick that incorporates this lick:

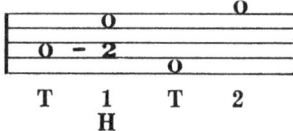

In this case the second string is picked simultaneously with the hammer-on.

Finally, try this popluar lick which can be used in many songs including "Foggy Mountain Breakdown". It involves bringing your right thumb all the way over to the second string. This isn't done very often in Scruggs style, but in this case it adds a lot of bounce to the lick. You'll be hammering on twice from the second to the third fret, and ending with a forward roll.

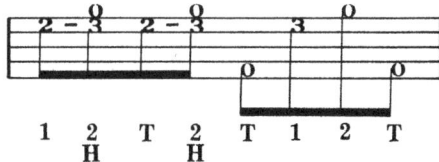

Once you've gotten these licks under your belt, you should be ready to put them into use. Here are versions of "Cripple Creek" and "Old Joe Clark" which make generous use of the three T 1 T 2 licks.

# Cripple Creek

Traditional
Arranged and adapted by Tony Trischka

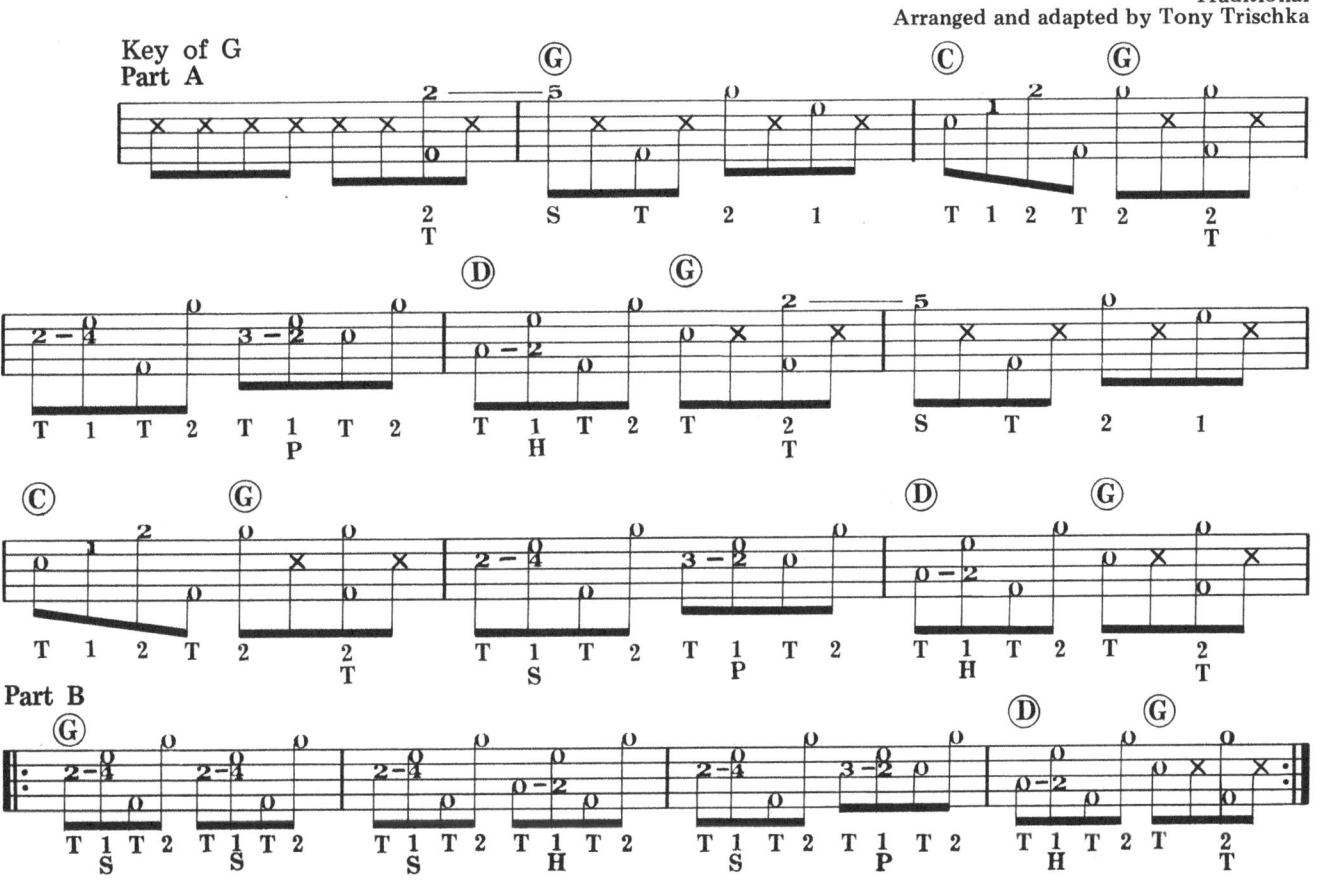

Larry McNeely and Charley Collins

# Old Joe Clark

Key of A
capo up two frets
Part A

Traditional
Arranged and adapted by Tony Trischka

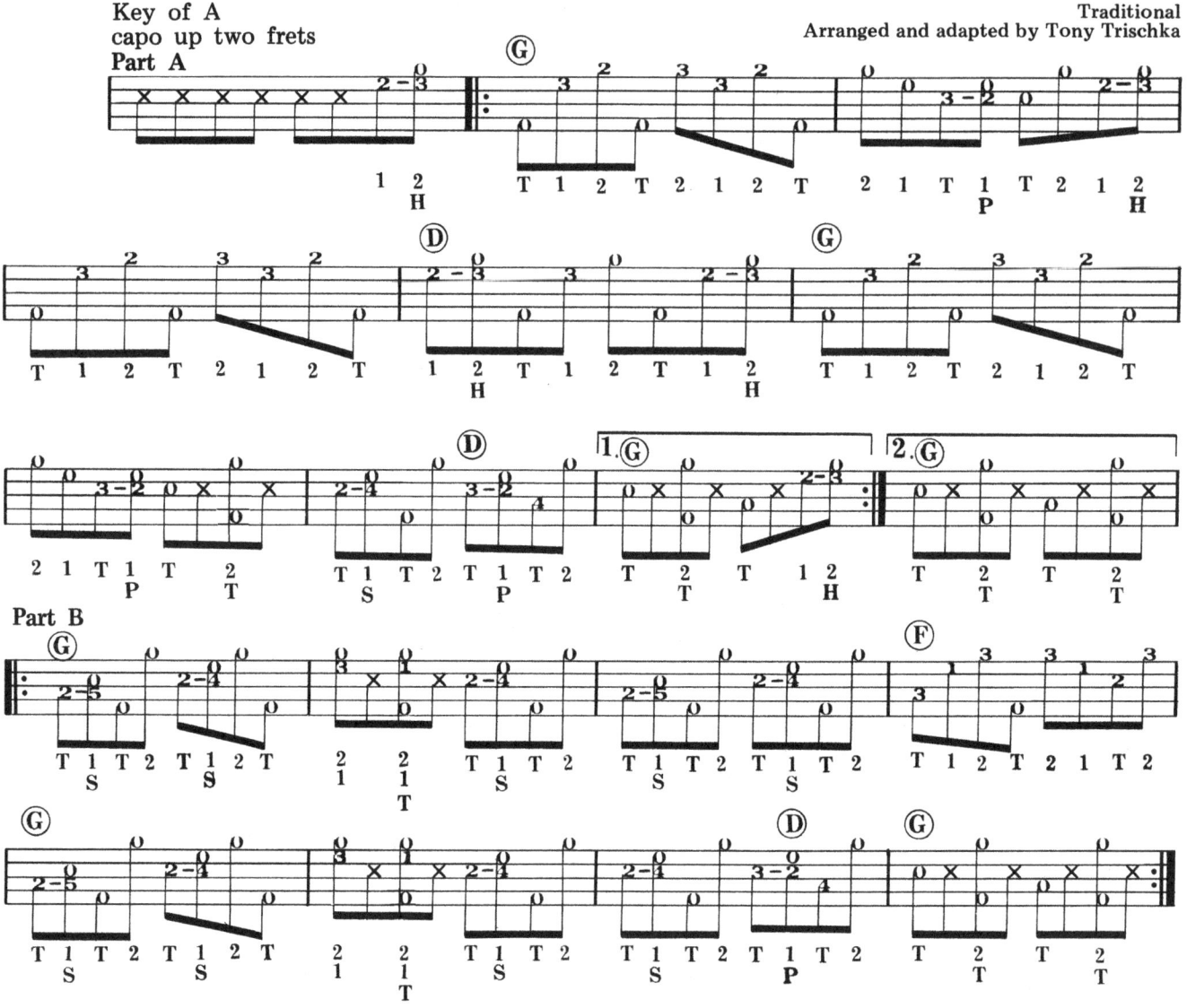

choking

This is a technique which is popular in bluegrass and blues music. To choke a string, simply fret it, then push it with the fretting finger to raise its pitch.

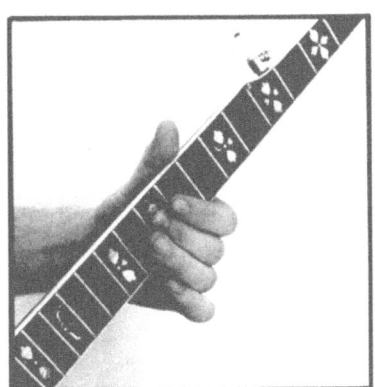

In tablature, a choke is indicated like this:

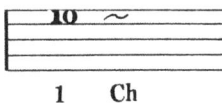

Here's an Earl Scruggs lick which expands on this idea:

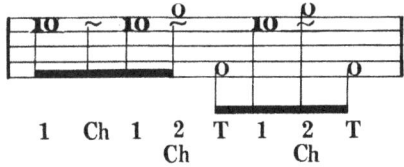

Choking is often used in the blues because it creates a feeling of tension. Listen to the playing of people like B. B. King and Eric Clapton and you'll see how true this is. Bill Monroe put a lot of the blues into his music when he was developing bluegrass—here's a lick that uses choking to get that sound:

harmonics

Harmonics are high-pitched tones that have a flute-like quality. You can get them by lightly touching a string at a certain point instead of pressing it down firmly against the fingerboard. Earl Scruggs has featured harmonics in his versions of "Bugle Call Rag" and "Foggy Mountain Chimes".

The most common point to produce harmonics on the banjo is at the twelfth fret, or halfway point of the string.

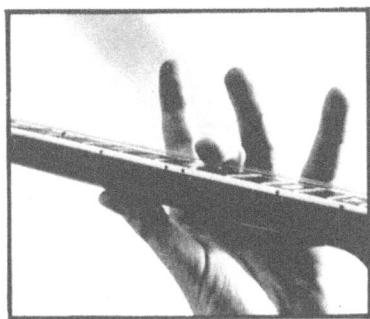

When you do this, you get a tone that's an octave above the open string. Here's a "bugle" sound to demonstrate. Remember, you should play the harmonic directly over the fret.

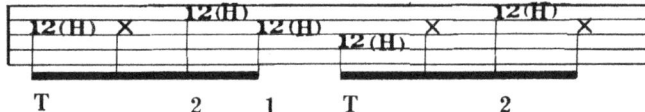

Since harmonics work on a mathematical basis, you can also find them at the "thirdway" points (seventh and nineteenth frets), and "quarterway" points (fifth fret and just beyond the fingerboard). If you go foraging on your own, you can find other less prominent, but still audible ones.

Here's an ending lick which puts harmonics to good use:

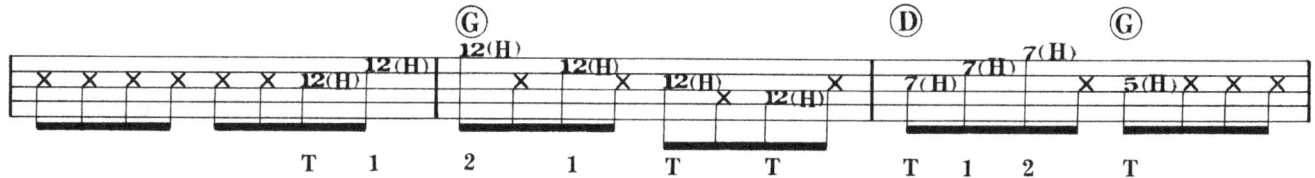

Although you usually play several harmonics in a row over one fret, you can also mix them up like this:

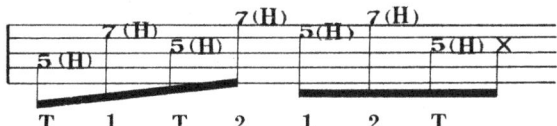

In addition, you can intersperse harmonics with the regular notes in your playing. Listen to my second break on "For You" from my *Bluegrass Light* album for an example.

Now that you've gone through this whirlwind introduction to Scruggs style banjo playing, you should be ready to move on. However, if you want a more in-depth study of the Scruggs approach, pick up a copy of Peter Wernick's *Bluegrass Banjo* (Oak Publications), or Earl Scruggs' own book published by Peer International.

# Reno Style

In the 1950s Don Reno devised a style which, for the first time, allowed the banjoist to play note-for-note melodies in a bluegrass setting. The technique he used was very similar to flat picking; but instead of using a flat pick, he alternated the thumb and index finger of his right hand to get the same effect. This next lick will give you a good idea of what he accomplished:

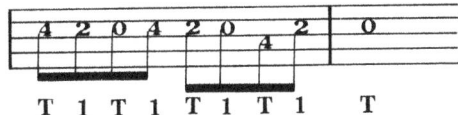

To get more of a feel for the Reno style, try this version of the A part to "Old Joe Clark":

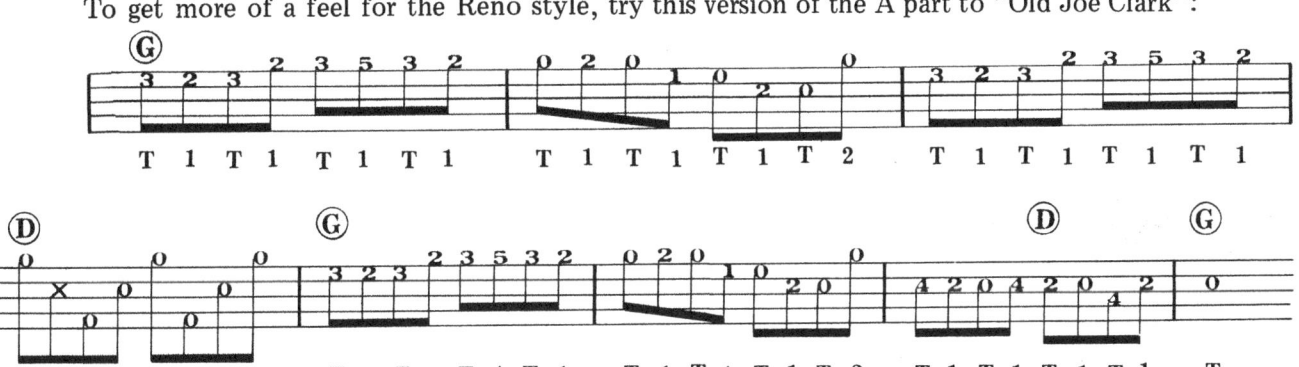

The sound you're getting here may seem a little bit choppy because in some cases, you're picking the same string several times in a row. This results in the damping of one note as you hit the next one. In cases where you want a hard, punchy sound, this choppiness can be an advantage. You'll almost feel like you can rip the strings right off the fingerboard. At other times, though, you may want a more flowing sound in the melody, especially if you want to play fiddle tunes; and this is where the melodic style comes in.

Don Reno

# The Melodic Style

Now we're ready to get into the heart of this book, the melodic style. For the first time you'll be able to play long, flowing note-for-note melodies with ease.

The key to the melodic style is the idea that you *never* pick the same string twice in a row. By alternating strings, many of them open, you can get a smooth, rolling sound.

Instead of playing,                you can play:

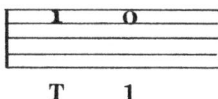 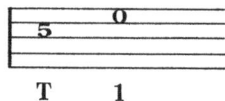

To expand on this idea, here are two versions of a G scale, the first done in the Reno style and the second, melodically. Notice that the Reno style only uses the thumb and index finger of the right hand, while the melodic style uses the thumb, index and middle fingers. This allows for greater versatility and speed in playing.

Reno style:

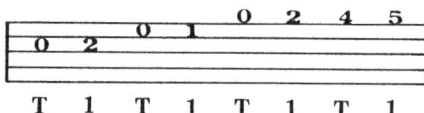

Melodic style:

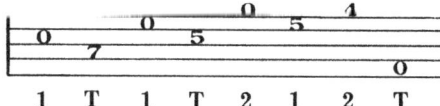

You'll find that when you fret a string in the melodic style, it's often higher in pitch than the next higher open string. For instance, the third string - fifth fret produces a higher note than the open second string. This phenomenon may be hard to get used to at first, but after a little bit of practice, it'll get much easier.

We've now compared the melodic approach to Reno picking, but how does it differ from Scruggs style? In the melodic style, most of the notes played are melody notes. Scruggs style, on the other hand, has its basis in chords, so it can only approximate the melody. This is especially true in the case of fiddle tunes. Listen to Scruggs' playing on "Sally Goodin" from *Foggy Mountain Banjo* (CS - 8364), and compare it to the version included on the record in this book. Scruggs only plays every third or fourth melody note, while the notes he puts in-between serve as embellishment. In the melodic version, all the melody notes are included and given equal clarity and importance.

Also, in Scruggs style the right hand usually emphasizes only the melody notes, while it skims over the others in a sort of chordal wash. In the melodic approach, where all the notes are part of the melody, the accents fall in a variety of places, depending on the mood of the musician and the nature of the tune. This all has to do with *dynamics*, or the stressing of one note or passage over another, in order to make the music more expressive.

One other difference between the two styles has to do with the role of the fifth string. Scruggs uses it mostly as a drone and rarely frets it except to add color to backup chords. In the melodic style, the fifth string is often fretted and becomes important as an equal carrier of the melody. Here's an example:

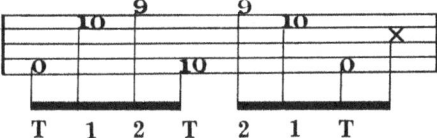

Before we get into heavy playing in the chapters ahead, I'd like to discuss one more thing with you—rhythm. Melodic playing involves a set of right hand rolls that aren't always found in Scruggs style, and until you get used to them your time may be a little shaky. For this reason I suggest that you work with a metronome. This will involve a certain amount of patience and discipline on your part; but if you can play along slowly with the metronome as you're learning new licks or songs and gradually work up to faster tempos, you'll find an amazing improvement in your rhythm. Remember, a steady rhythm is one of the most important elements you can have in your playing.

In the next chapter you'll learn more right hand rolls, plus new left hand positions. In addition, you'll see exactly how Bill Keith, one of the two developers of the melodic approach, came up with his style.

# Bill Keith

In 1961, a young Bill Keith went to the Philadelphia Folk Festival to enter its prestigious banjo contest. His melodic versions of "Devil's Dream" and "Sailor's Hornpipe" won him first prize and a chance to play his tunes in the evening concert. This was undoubtedly the first time that the melodic style had been played in front of a large, knowledgable audience.

The real turning point, though, came in 1963, when Bill spent nine months as one of Bill Monroe's *Bluegrass Boys*. On records and in live appearances with Monroe, he introduced this exciting new melodic sound to a great number of people.

Although the basic techniques Bill used weren't original (they can be traced far back in classical guitar literature), he was the first person that most people heard applying them to bluegrass banjo. In actuality, Bobby Thompson had been independently working on the same idea a couple of years earlier. However, Bill was the one who got it out to the public in large doses, and for this reason his name became most closely associated with the style.

When I interviewed Bill for this book, he discussed the influences and thought processes that led to the development of *Keith style* banjo playing. So in his own words, and mine, here's how it all unfolded:

"One inspiration was that Don Reno lick from the chorus of 'Banjo Signal.'"

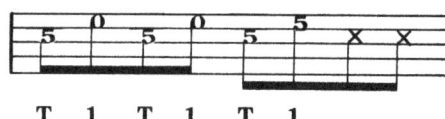

"The other thing came from Don Stover's playing."

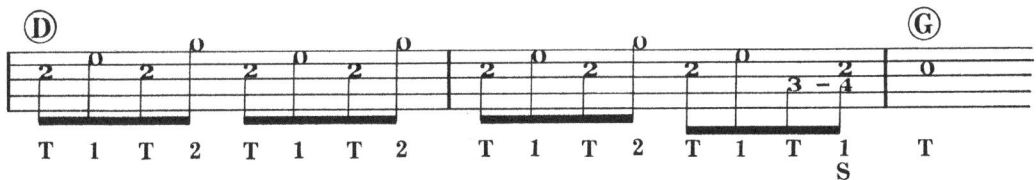

"And anyway, that turned into this":

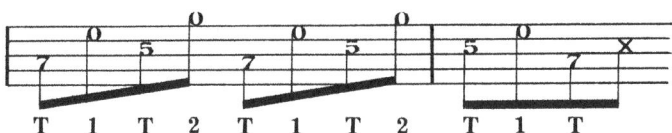

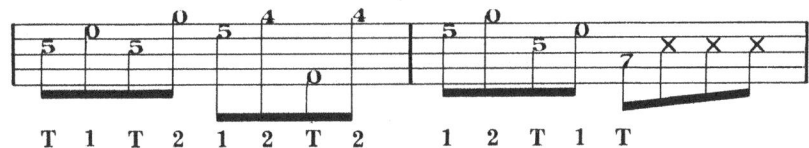

(These are actually just melodic fragments, and aren't intended as licks. Instead, they show how the Reno and Stover licks were expanded into the rudiments of the melodic style.)

"Then a couple of weeks later I figured out that you could get:

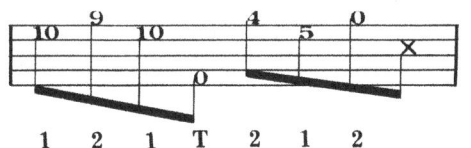 and then this":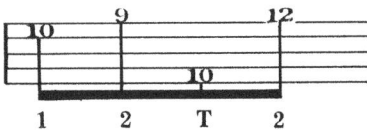

At this point, Bill realized that these fragments were actually sections of scales, the use of which could open up a whole new area for musical exploration. To move into this realm, Bill had to come up with a fresh approach to the fingerboard, which meant getting used to new left hand positions and right hand rolls.

Since scales are so important to the melodic style, try working through these. They're the ones which are most commonly used as the basis for melodic licks and fiddle tunes. You should start off slowly, working until you feel comfortable with what you're playing; then gradually build up speed. As I mentioned before, it may help you to play with a metronome to solidify the timing in your right hand (for a more detailed description of scales, look at Appendix 1).

### G scale (one octave)

### G scale (two octaves)
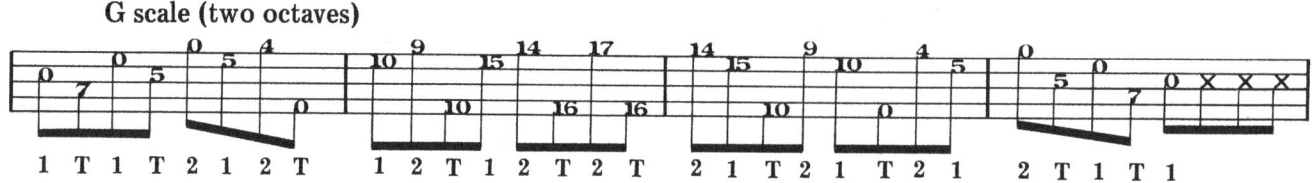

### D scale (two octaves)
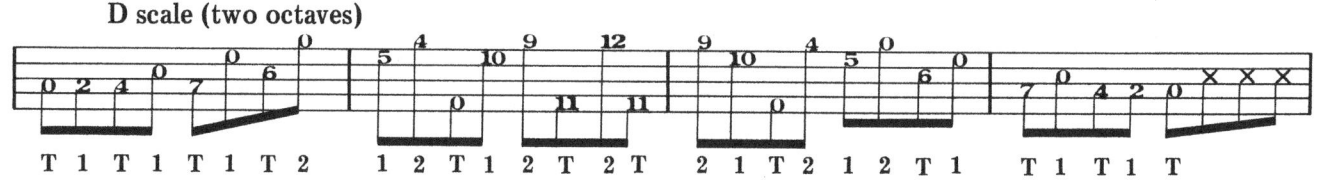

### C scale
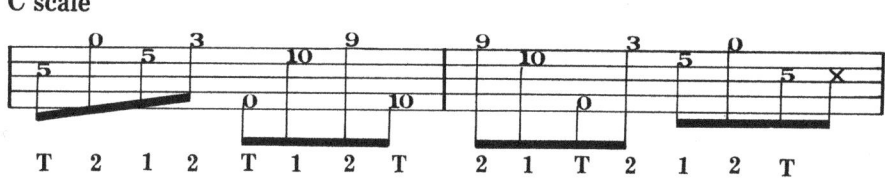

### A scale
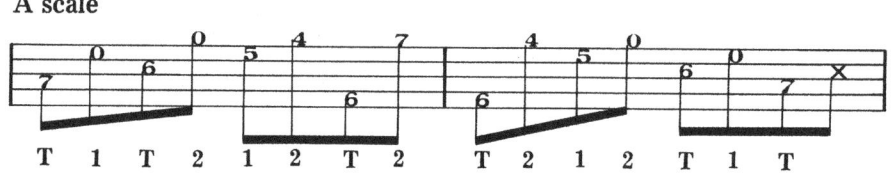

### A7 scale
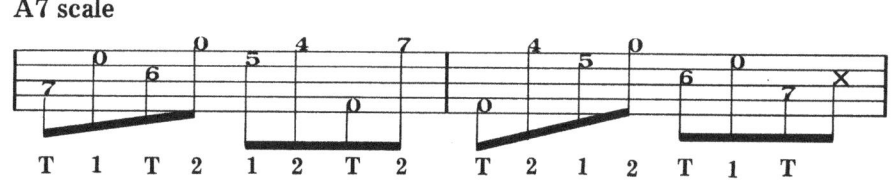

If you look at the first few notes of the D scale you'll see that the Reno style has been used. This is because there is no other way you can play consecutive notes on the first four frets of the fourth string.

Now that you've gone through a few scales you can put them to practical use. Here's how Bill applied them to his music: "The first use I made of this technique to play licks like this was:

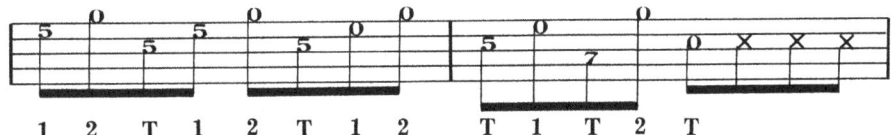

and

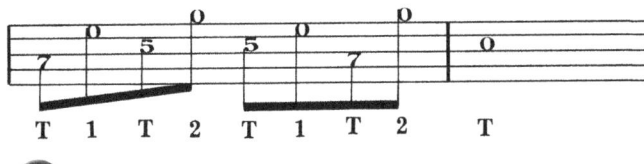

Both of these runs fit nicely into this melodic version of "Cripple Creek":

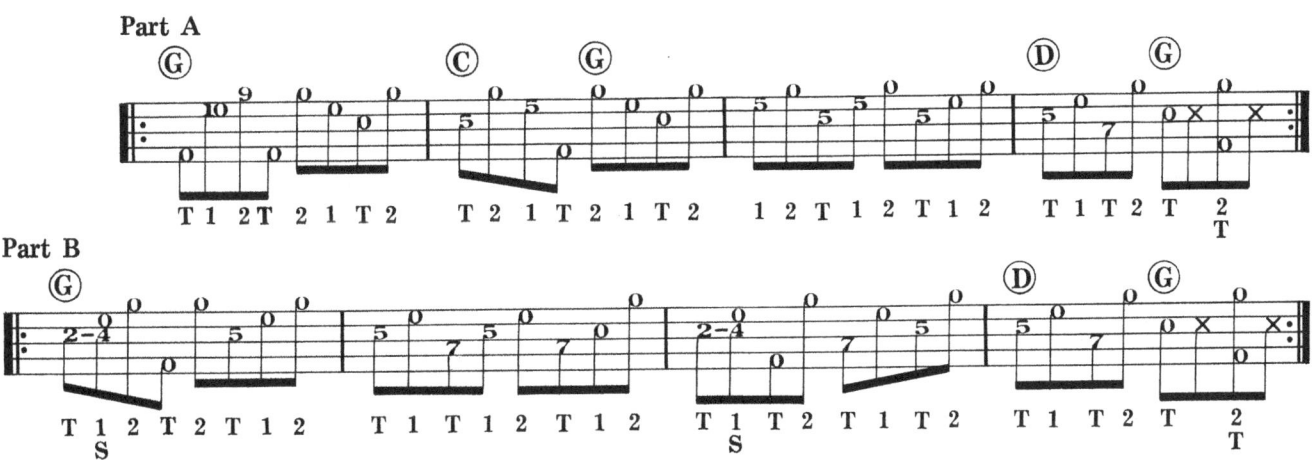

Bill describes how he worked up another lick which is closely identified with his style: "I got a tape of this guy Noah Crase who played 'Noah's Breakdown' and it was a tape, recorded off the radio. It drifted in and out. Classic long distance reception. And I swear in there he was doing something out of this position (basically a D7)":

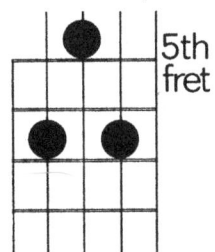

"I've always had a pretty good ear for recognizing positions and so I found this lick which happened to fit into the space":

This is very satisfying to play because of its economy of movement. The left hand hardly moves at all; and here's pretty much the same lick taken down two frets:

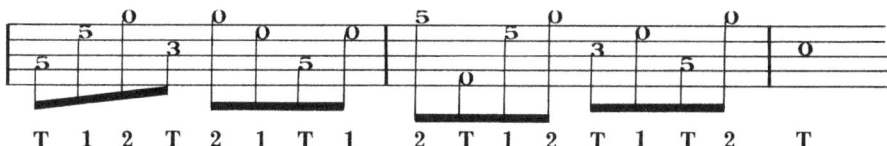

"When I saw Noah Crase years later he was in fact using those positions, although I don't know what his right hand roll was. But in fact it was very close to that. But almost anything you do in that position ... works to a certain extent":

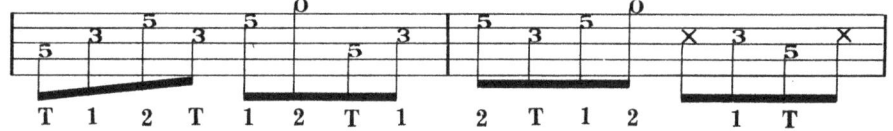

If you can get hold of Keith and Rooney's *Living on the Mountain* (Prestige Folklore 14002), listen to Bill's melodic break to "Salty Dog." It includes a version of the first D7 lick mentioned above, plus several other useful runs.

As Bill's style gradually progressed, he felt less motivated to throw in the long runs and started moving toward a more subtle, syncopated use of melodic fragments: "The more I played with Bill Monroe, the less it seemed that some of that stuff worked as ornaments to a tune. I mean it was great to use for leads. But just to throw in a lot of licks and splash it up seemed wrong. So I was using less and less of that as time went on." Here's a really tasteful syncopated passage to demonstrate:

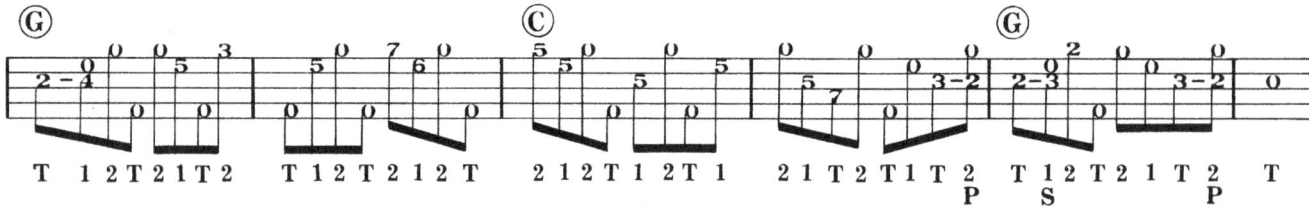

The ultimate example of this idea is his break in "New Camptown Races," which features the complete fusion of the Scruggs and melodic styles. Several licks from this tune became banjo standards overnight, including this next one. It isn't strictly melodic, but it's very interesting because of its shifting contours and beautiful right hand syncopation.

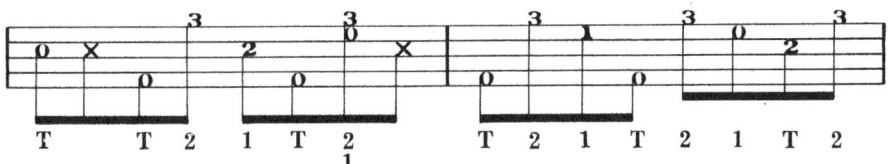

One other aspect of Bill's playing that stands out is his fantastic right hand work. He combines an absolutely solid sense of rhythm with a driving and syncopated attack, both of which help to make his style all the more delectable. Here he talks about some of the people who have influenced this phase of his music: "I think Allen Shelton has a beautiful surge and bounce to the way he plays, and so does Don Stover. I spent a lot of time listening to both of them, in addition to Earl, and I think it's really an important part of playing to me. It shouldn't be flat and non-rhythmic."

Now for the dessert. Here are a few melodic endings which Bill used to good advantage with Bill Monroe. Try them and then see if you can come up with some of your own, using what you've learned in the last few pages.

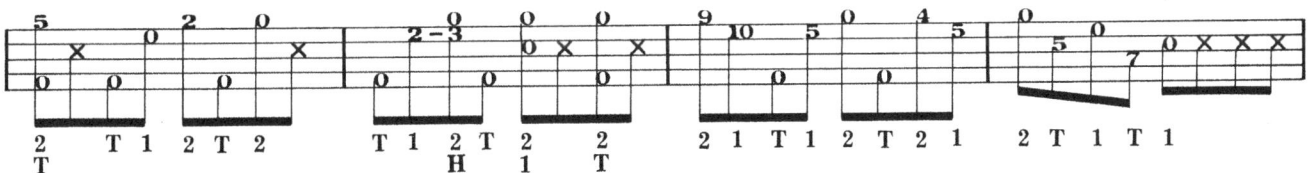

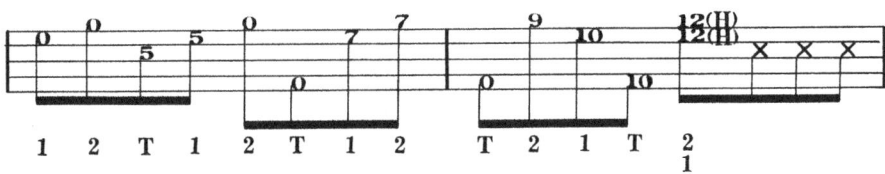

These endings are just further proof of Bill's complete inventiveness. When you realize that he set a totally new direction for the banjo, and when you think of the number of people who have followed him down this path, you can easily see why he's considered such a giant in the bluegrass field.

# Blackberry Blossom

Traditional
Arranged and adapted by Bill Keith

As played on *Festival*, Vanguard Records VRS-9225

## Little Sadie

Traditional
Arranged and adapted by Bill Keith

Key of Dm
tuning : ADFAD

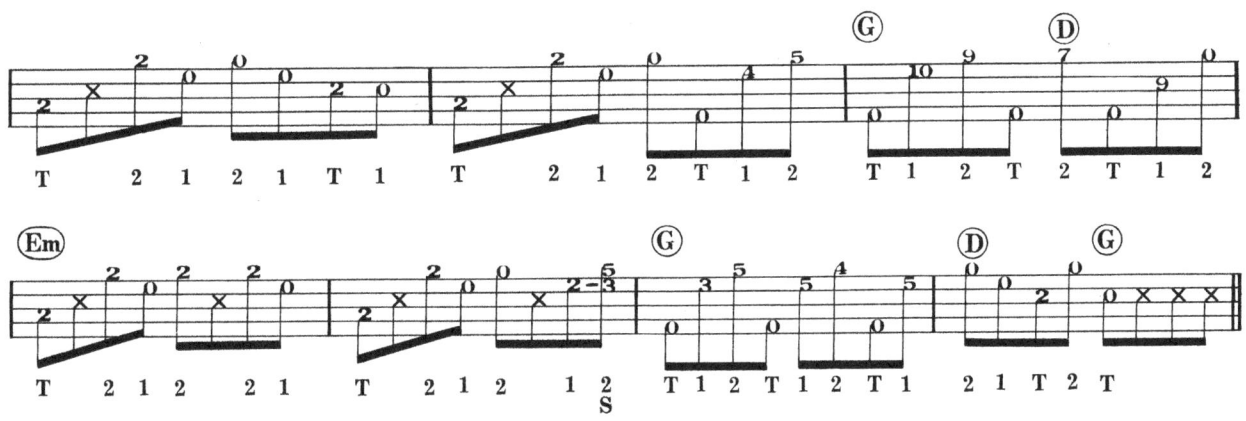

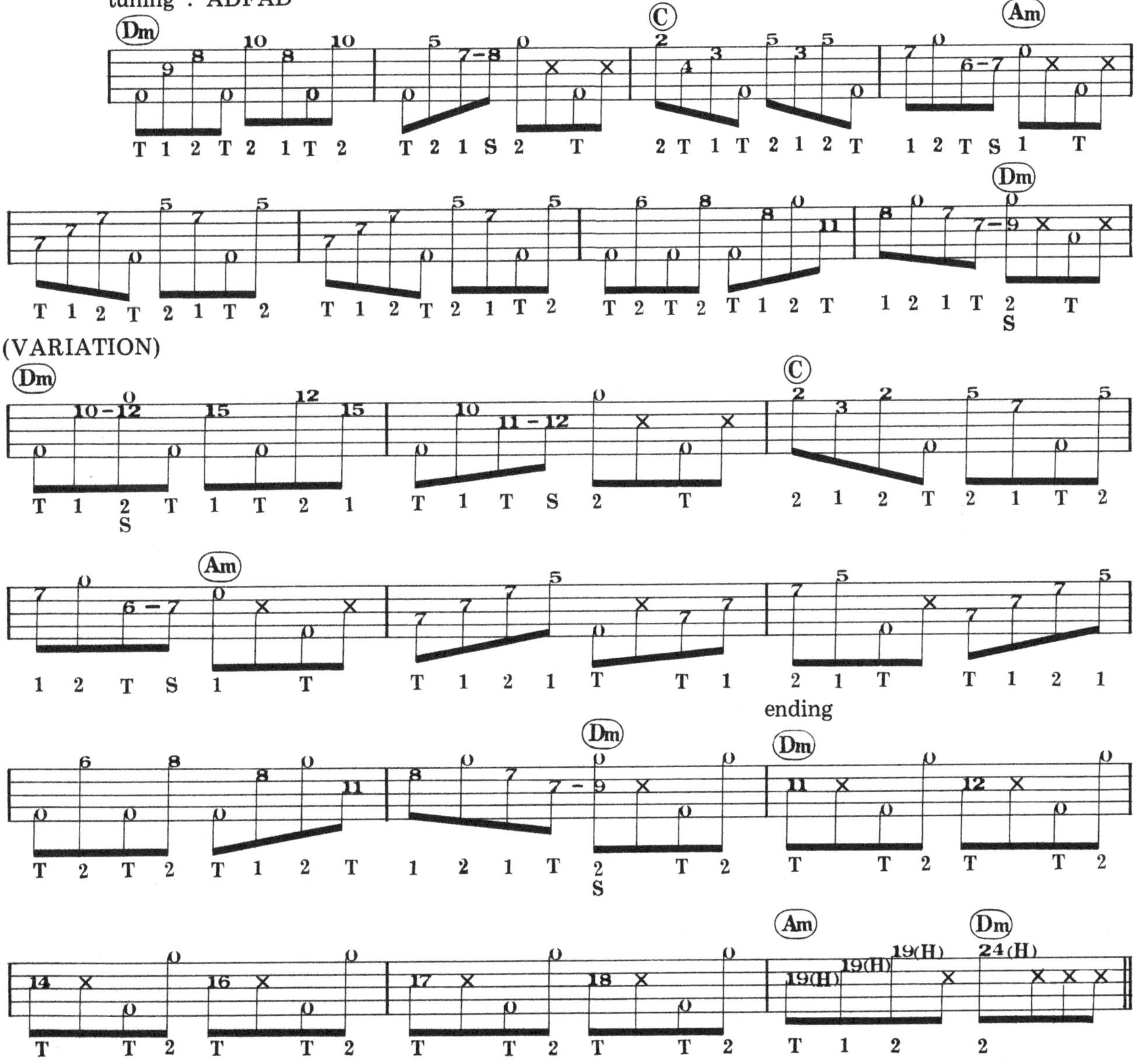

© Floridian Music, 1969. All Rights Reserved. Used by Permission.

As played on *Sweet Moments* by the Blue Velvet Band, Warner Brothers 1802

# Arkansas Traveler

Key of G
Part A

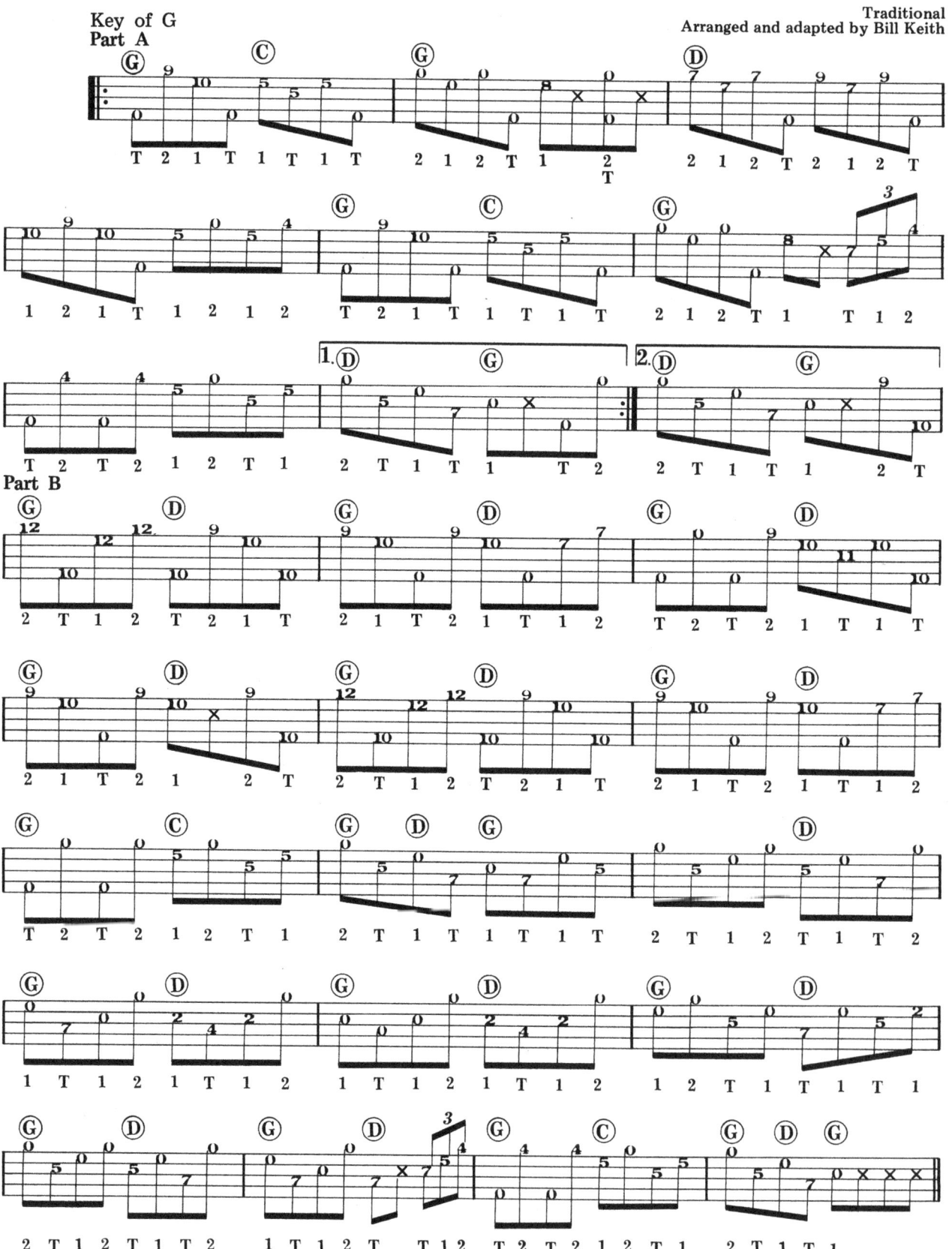

As played on *Festival*, Vanguard Records VRS-9225

## "NEW CAMPTOWN RACES"

*Tony:* How did you first get into incorporating the melodic style into songs such as "New Camptown Races" which, instead of being either all melodic or all Scruggs, is a combination of the two?

*Bill:* Well, basically I started off using phrases or pieces of scales or rearrangements of pieces of scales as ornaments. Then I got more into playing fiddle tunes or someone else's tunes using that. But basically those were all worked out as things to play. Whereas it was more of an improvisatory style when you were just using a piece here and there. And so tunes fall somewhere on a scale, meaning that you can either render all or some of them in that very imitable style. I mean a tune like "New Camptown Races" works out so that a lot of it seems to come out. But that's really a created melody, in a way, compared to the way Frank (Wakefield) is playing. It's an approximation of the melody as the style permits, depending on how much forethought you put into it.

*The Muleskinner Band/L to R: Clarence White, Bill Keith, David Grisman, Peter Rowan and Richard Greene*

# New Camptown Races

© Wynwood Music Company, Inc., 1968. All Rights Reserved. Used by Permission.

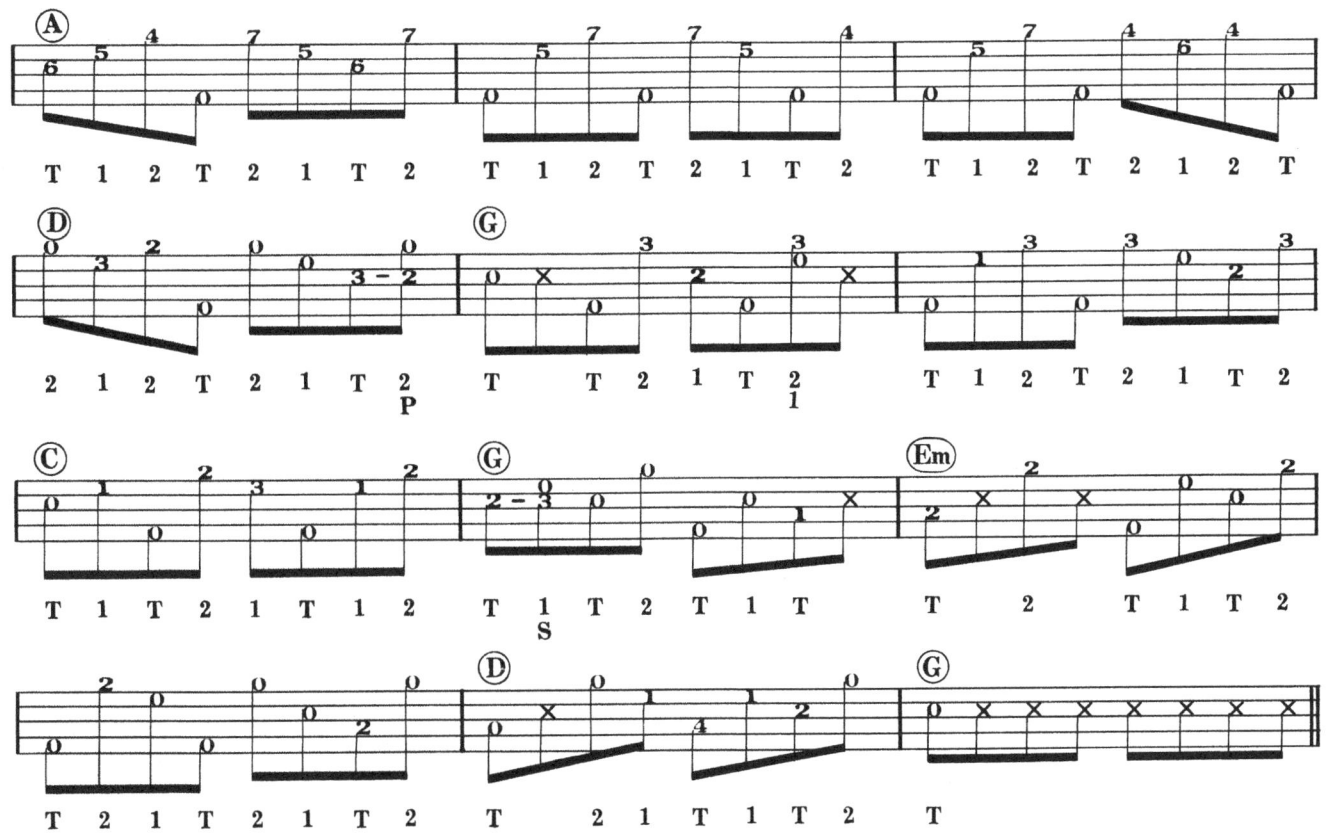

As played on *Red Allen, Frank Wakefield and the Kentuckians*, Folkways FA 2408

# Opus 57 In G Minor

Key of Gm  
Capo up three frets  
Introduction

Dave Grisman

© Zut Music, 1974. All Rights Reserved. Used by Permission.

Part B

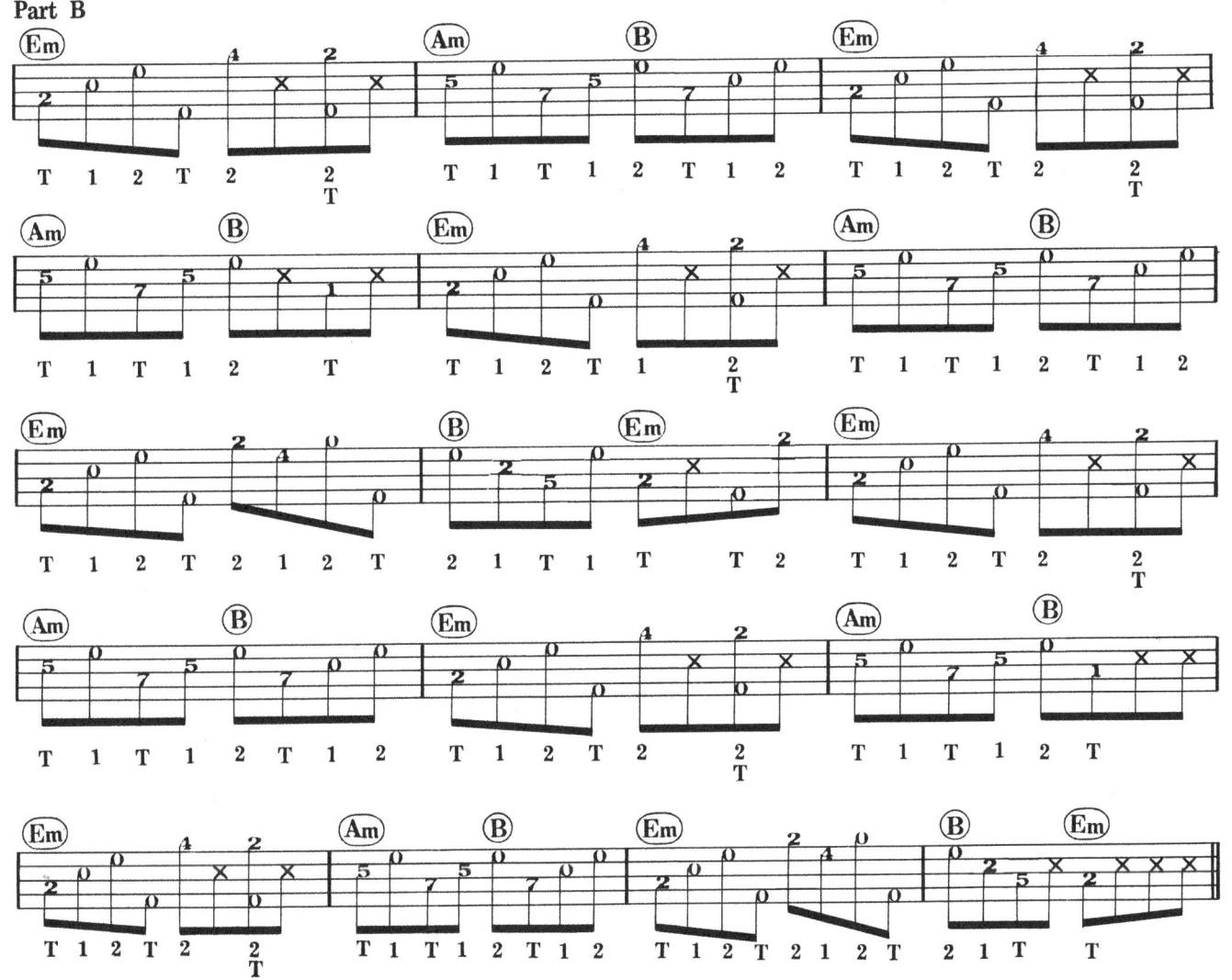

As played on *Muleskinner*, Warner Brothers Records BS 2787

41

# INTERVIEW WITH BILL KEITH

Tony: When did you start playing the banjo?

Bill: Well, I started playing four-string banjo, tenor, you know, when I was in about the fourth grade.

T: Did you play any other instruments?

B: I had taken piano lessons for a few years, but I didn't like them except for the last year. During that time I learned a lot about chord theory and chord construction, scale things which were sort of the basis of the operation.

T: Was there any one inspiring force that got you interested in five-string banjo?

B: I guess it was hearing the *Weavers* during the folk song revival. And at that point I'd already been playing for years and playing at square dances with the four-string banjo. So there were some tunes like "Old Joe Clark" and others that I recognized but hadn't tried to play. I played rhythm on the tenor and a little chord lead ... melody lead chords. But no single string thing with a flat pick. And I guess it was hearing Pete Seeger on the *Weavers* records and seeing the *Weavers* and Seeger in person and hearing the things on record that I wanted to be able to play on the banjo that were almost impossible to do on a four-string. So I bought a five-string for $15.

T: How old were you at that point?

B: I guess I was seventeen or eighteen. I remember it because I was a freshman in college when I first heard Pete Seeger and I bought my banjo in the fall of freshman year. And that was in 1957.

T: So did you get the Pete Seeger book and start working out of that?

B: Yes I did. It was the yellow edition. And as you know it didn't have much of the Scruggs style in it. In fact, "Cindy" was about the only thing in there. And in it, the use of the thumb is limited to the fifth string. So that's the way I thought they did it. And he said in there, go out and get some Earl Scruggs records ... some Don Reno records, and so I did. But meanwhile, I couldn't wait to get to the back of the book where the interesting strums were. You know, the rhumba and flamenco. But I got the records anyway. And I didn't really like the bluegrass thing very much at that point. It took me about two weeks to get over my dislike of it, or at least until I realized what the melody was, and where, and so on; I didn't dig it a whole lot the first time I heard it. Gee, I don't know. I got the Don Reno records, too, a little later, and I dug them a lot more on the first hearing than I did later.

T: Ultimately you learned all the Scruggs stuff note-for-note.

B: Yeah. I thought he was a pretty good model. I thought Scruggs played with the kind of taste that was really good, and a lot of techniques which weren't played to show off the technique per se. I mean, "Dixie Breakdown" may seem hard, but obviously it's very easy compared to some contortions Scruggs had to do with his right hand. I guess I was less worried about what my left hand had to do when I was learning the five-string because I had already played the tenor and plectrum banjo. So I didn't worry about my left hand as much, and I paid a lot of attention to the right. So that may have something to do with why Scruggs struck me as a good model.

T: Do you want to talk a little bit more about right hand techniques while we're on the subject?

B: Yeah, well here's my current thesis of what you should be able to do with your right hand. First you lay out every possible lick—it doesn't take very much time to write out every possible combination—and then of all those, a lot are very useful. But all of them should be fluent, because only when everything is of a very similar degree of difficulty can you change from one roll to another in mid-thought. So you have every possible direction, everything down, second nature.

T: How did you come up with "Devil's Dream?"

B: A neighbor's wife plays the fiddle, and I used to go down there Wednesday nights and play banjo to her fiddle and it just occurred to me that it should be possible. So I worked out the "Devil's Dream." Then for a long time I didn't put the technique to use on any other tunes.
T: So you just had that worked up, and that was about it?
B: Well, then I got "Sailor's Hornpipe" together.
T: What year was this?
B: The first recording of "Devil's Dream" was in '62, I think.
T: Eric Weissberg and Marshall Brickman had a version of it out also around the same time. What was the story behind that?
B: Well, I'd heard Eric and Marshall play before and they were both Scruggsophiles, although having sort of an urban twist to their playing anyway. Certainly harmonically they were both very advanced in that way. But I'd never heard them play anything like that ("Devil's Dream"). Both of them were in town, with the *Tarriers*, and they came into the Club 47 where Jim Rooney and I were playing. We played our medley... our big instrumental. And I think we played it once a set at that point. We were really doing it often. And they heard it and looked at each other. And then a couple of months later they had this record out.

Bill Keith and Jim Rooney

T: This was before you had your record out?
B: Yeah, it was. We recorded it in September or October of that year (1962). I think we recorded just after I returned from serving Uncle Sam. Anyway, they had their record out a little before us.
T: So you came up with "Devil's Dream" around 1961?
B: I believe I had played that by Christmas of 1960. And during the summer I played music, and then in the fall, back at school (Amherst), there was no band to work with. However, later I did work with *Wynn Fay and the Ridgerunners* out of Belchertown (Massachusetts). I rode down the main street on a bale of hay which is only the first of two times I've experienced that in a wagon. Learn what suspension systems are all about. But I think it was during that fall that I got a lot of this together.

T: How did you come to meet Bobby Thompson?
B: Steve[1] met him before I did and said, "Hey, you gotta meet this guy." And we went down to Converse, South Carolina, and listened and hung out a little bit. He had played with *Jim and Jesse* by that time. But he was in the army, I think, welding or something. So we played some, and then we came back up here, and I had taped it.
T: So you and Bobby Thompson had developed along the same lines independently of each other?
B: Well, I guess. Except there's one point that I've never been very clear on. And this was after I'd been working with Bill Monroe and we'd played the "Devil's Dream," "Santa Claus," "Salt Creek" and "Shenandoah Breakdown," and "Pike County Breakdown," which we recorded but which was never released. I think we did play it on the Opry.

Bill Monroe, Bill Keith and Del McCoury

And a lot of the tunes Monroe played I'd throw my licks into. Gee, I don't know. I can't understand that he's not digging some of this on the radio. This has never been very clear to me. I had heard my *Jim and Jesse* records from past years and had learned "Border Ride" and the break to "Dixie Hoedown." And it's really nice. So I admit to having been influenced by him. And it doesn't seem likely that he escaped some influence from me if he was listening to the Opry.
T: I'm sure it was a cross thing. I mean, you went down and taped him and learned some of his songs.
B: Yeah, but that was after having worked with Bill. It was a good eight months after I'd quit working with Bill. And so it was over a year after I'd first started working with Bill that I first met Bobby. That's about the way the chronology goes, although I didn't hear any of his playing after his recordings with *Jim and Jesse.*
T: When you went down South to see him in 1964 with Steve Arkin, was he playing any of your licks?

---

[1] Steve Arkin—played with Bill Monroe just after Bill Keith did and heard Bobby Thompson at this time.

B: No. Not to a measurable degree. He was playing a lot of jazz-type tunes that Allen Shelton[2] was also. He was very much into Alan Shelton. Not to underline the point too heavily, but during the time I was playing with Bill Monroe I was not influenced by Bobby Thompson to any extent. I have to feel that it was my stuff at that point.
T: What sort of influence did Monroe have on you?
B: That's a long story. He never really would spell things out. But when he was pleased with the way things sounded you could tell. And so obviously you're trying to play something that turns him on, and you just try different things and you seem to notice what works; a lot of the time what works is just real straight, hard-driving . . . which doesn't mean uncomplicated. But it doesn't mean loaded with flowery fills and phrases. He's very much into a lot of rhythmic things which is a great right hand challenge anyway. Although a lot of them can sound real simple. Like "Santa Claus" (from Monroe's *Bluegrass Instrumentals*), for example, was completely upbeat. He wanted to have it that way. In fact every other time he played it, except the time we were in the studio that day when it was recorded, it was upbeats he was playing it in. And I copied the rhythm in my banjo break from what he was doing on the mandolin. And then so did the fiddle. And so when we got to the studio he said, "Well, I'm not going to do it. Everybody else is doing it."
T: Did you learn lots of fiddle tunes from him?
B: He played a lot of them. But his style is not as explicit about notes of tunes as, say, Bobby Osborne, for example, when he plays a fiddle tune. I didn't learn a lot of fiddle tunes note-for-note as I believe Larry McNeely did from Howdy Forrester. I think he lived with Howdy Forrester for a while when he was in Nashville working for Roy Acuff, and learned dozens, if not hundreds, of tunes from Big Howdy. I never did that with Bill.
T: He approximates the melody most of the time; plays at it.
B: Yeah. Not a lot of what you'd call neat little turns like the fiddle would do. I mean, they're more of a very personal blues-interpreted slurring of notes.
T: In more recent years it seems like you've been getting more into a chordal thing. After you left Bill you went to the *Jim Kweskin Jug Band* where you played more of a chordal style. Was that going back to your tenor days?
B: I suppose it was. I always liked that music. I played five-string for a little bit in the band when I first started. Then I realized that that really wasn't what that band needed. I still got off, and I still do, on that style. And at that time I just really wanted to do that. It was a very tenor-plectrum type of thing. Although nothing else that I learned hurt. I learned a lot of other new left hand positions. It's funny. During the time of the *Jug Band* I learned a hell of a lot about chords and chord motion that I probably wouldn't have learned if I had stayed in a straight bluegrass band.
T: What do you see as a future direction for the banjo? It's gone from melodic into chromatic. . . .
B: I like the distinction, by the way. I never considered what I played very chromatic.
T: Then how would you describe your playing?
B: Well, I guess melodic is the better term. I try to play melodic things. Passing chords do involve notes that sometimes are chromatic to the scale, to the key of the music. But even so, melodic style as I started using it was more relative to the very simple melodies of fiddle tunes. And there aren't very many fiddle tunes that have what you'd call chromatic notes. Many more people, including you, Tony, are responsible for a lot more developments in chromatic playing than I have been.
T: Well, you set the groundwork for the whole thing. You opened it up for everyone.
B: Well, I don't know; we were talking about records and history, and other people had records of it out before I did.

---

[2] A former banjoist for *Jim and Jesse*.

T: Who else?

B: Eric's record was out. Bobby Thompson's things were out. I think Doug Dillard had recorded a version of "Cripple Creek." I don't remember when that came out. But I heard the record when I was living in Washington, which was after we made this record but not after it had been out for long. I think it was just being able to play with Bill Monroe and playing on the Opry a lot, and making some records, and playing all over the country....

T: That spread the word.

B: Right.

T: You seem to have an unusual right hand technique. You brought in a lot of syncopation compared to what was being done.

B: I always tried to do that. Though it's funny. Scruggs does some nice things with it. And Reno does also, but sort of by approaching it from the other direction. Multiples of three don't fit into multiples of eight very easily unless there's some syncopation involved.

T: It seems that you tried to incorporate this into your own style.

B: Well, I tried to do it with what I learned from Scruggs too, because if I hadn't learned a lot of his right hand stuff, then I never would have been prepared to play any melodic things. And so it all has to work in there together. But along the way you can get hung up on the body of tunes that emphasize that style and then let the harmonic considerations slide. That's why I really enjoyed the years in the *Jug Band*. Because, although I didn't play bluegrass to any degree for something like four years there, I did learn something about other forms of music like blues and electric music.

T: It opened your eyes to a lot of different things.

B: Right.

L to R: Bessie Lee Mauldin, Billy Baker, Bill Monroe, Bill Keith and Del McCoury

# Melodic Blues Runs

The Blues has always played an important role in bluegrass, but its application to the banjo has traditionally been limited to a small number of licks. However, with the advent of the melodic style, this situation has become a thing of the past. Now you can jump all over the neck, playing a myriad of blues runs with ease.

Bobby Thompson (featured in the next chapter) is the one who is usually given credit for coming up with this concept. He simply took the standard blues scale,

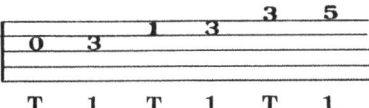

and applied it to the melodic style. To do this he had to find other positions up the neck that would allow him to play these same blues notes. You'll find that if you're playing in the key of G, a lot of these notes can be found in the B♭ and F chords, and that these positions,

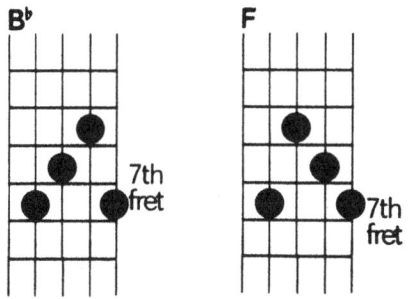

are the ones most commonly used for blues runs. This makes sense because the two key notes in a blues scale are the flatted 3rd and the flatted 7th. In the key of G, these turn out to be the B♭ and F notes respectively. (Turn to the chord chart in Appendix 1 if this explanation confuses you.) Now let's see how this works in practice. Try this simple melodic run:

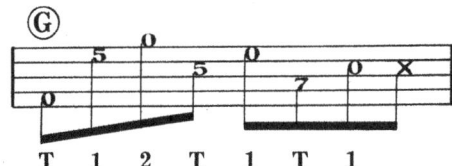

If you take the second note and move it up one fret (from an E to an F note) it suddenly takes on a bluesy feel. (Notice that the position created by the fretted notes is basically an F chord.)

Here's another blues run that is based on an eighth fret B♭ chord.

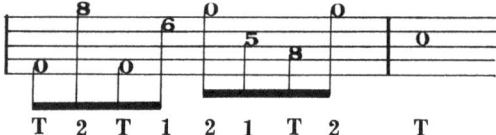

Besides flatted 3rd and 7th notes, flatted 5th notes also fit nicely into the blues sound. This next run takes you farther up the neck and has as its first note the flatted 5th. (In the key of G, D is the fifth, so a flatted 5th would be D♭ or C♯.)

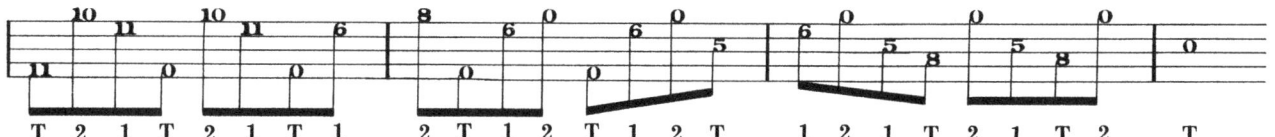

Notice the systematic motion which serves as a framework for this run. Throughout, you find yourself playing four descending notes, jumping back three, going down the next four, back another three, and so on until you reach the bottom. This kind of movement is very characteristic of a lot of melodic blues runs, and can be applied to other scales as well. Bill Keith's introduction to "Opus 57 in G Minor" is a perfect example of this.

When you first get into these long systematic runs, you may have some trouble synchronizing your right hand with your left because the rolls which are involved continually force your right hand to change direction in midstream to get the desired notes. In a way, then, your right hand is a slave of the left; but as your vocabulary of these runs increases, you'll find that your right hand will gradually get used to the unexpected. So just be patient and it *will* come to you.

One other point  melodic blues runs are very versatile. You can often play one run against three or four different chords. Take this lick:

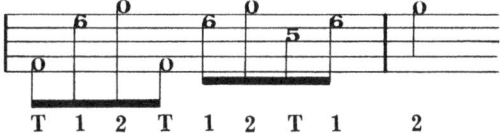

Although you would normally play a G chord behind it, a C, F or B♭ chord also works. This is because the notes involved take on a different meaning depending on their context. The second note, for instance, is an F note. If you're playing a G chord, the F is the seventh degree of the scale, which makes for musical compatability. With a C chord the F becomes the fourth degree, another nice fit. Against an F it's the tonic or I note, and so on. The other blues notes also sound good when played against a variety of chords. So you can really get a lot of mileage out of these runs if you're on your toes.

# Bobby Thompson

If you've ever heard the theme to "Hee Haw" on television or any number of country hits from Nashville, you've heard Bobby Thompson's brilliant banjo work. Until fairly recently though, Bobby had been somewhat of a legend whose work could only be heard on the records of Carl Story and *Jim and Jesse* from the late 1950s. Even back then, his remarkable drive and syncopation stood out. Also, he was beginning to incorporate the newborn melodic style into his playing. Unfortunately, the public wasn't ready for his innovations:

'When I left Carl and joined *Jim and Jesse*, when I'd play one of those tunes on stage, they'd just look at me like, "What in the world are you doing?"—so I just quit. Everybody had just heard Scruggs and Reno in those days, and anything else just blew by them. I was kind of discouraged. I just played one break like that on record with *Jim and Jesse*, "Border Ride," I think. But I just stuck to the Scruggs stuff. The other stuff, I just let it slide. Just stuff I'd pick in the back seat.'

'I don't think *Jim and Jesse* had anything against it, it was just that on stage it wasn't accepted. You could work on one of those things six months and they'd just sit there, but play "Foggy Mountain Breakdown" and it would tear the house down.'[3]

---

[3] Quote courtesy of *Bluegrass Unlimited*.

Actually, Bobby had recorded two songs with *Jim and Jesse* which contained the rudiments of melodic playing, "Border Ride" and "Dixie Hoedown." Due to copyright problems, I can't include examples from these songs, and the Starday records on which these tunes originally appeared are out of print now. So you'll have to track down a friend or relative who has either *Stars of the Grand Ole Opry* (SLP-365) to hear "Border Ride," or one of the old Starday sampler records for "Dixie Hoedown." The *Stars* album combines two of the all-time great bluegrass bands separately on one record—*Flatt and Scruggs* from the early '50s, and the late '50s *Jim and Jesse*. The *Jim and Jesse* cuts feature incredible singing from the McReynolds brothers and solid instrumental work not only from Bobby, but also from a young fiddler named Vassar Clements.

Since those glory days with *Jim and Jesse*, Bobby's melodic style has evolved into a highly refined form. For all its sophistication and precision, though, it contains an inner quality of raw power, so when Bobby starts a break it feels like potential energy is about to explode in all directions. He applies this controlled strength not only to standard melodic licks, but also to the melodic blues runs which he almost singlehandedly brought into existence: "I just got into them working up something Jerry Reed had out that had a bunch of blues runs in it. It was just like opening up a new door, a new feel."

Bobby uses blues notes in a wide variety of contexts, from long winding runs to short spicy fragments. Here's one of his medium length licks which can make for a dramatic entrance or ending to a solo:

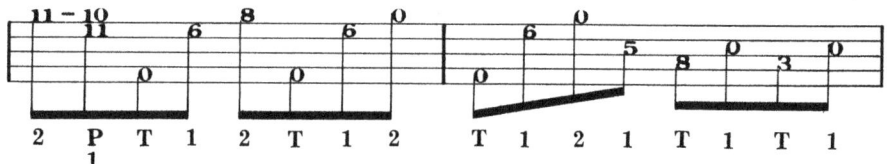

This next passage, from the A part of "Devil Dance," expands on this idea:

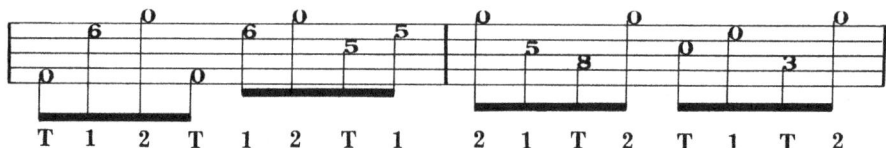

The nice touch here is the contrast between the overall blues feel and the inclusion of the two major sounding notes at the end of the first measure. Although these two notes make up a small part of the tune, by being there they give the blues notes a lot more impact. Tasty details like this are commonplace in Bobby's playing, and you can't help but get the impression that every nuance of his music is taken into consideration in advance, either on a conscious or subliminal level.

Bobby also brings his style to bear on descending runs which aren't necessarily in the blues mode. For instance, look at the first six bars of "Foxfire" to see how he dissects major scales.

Here's another handy run in that style:

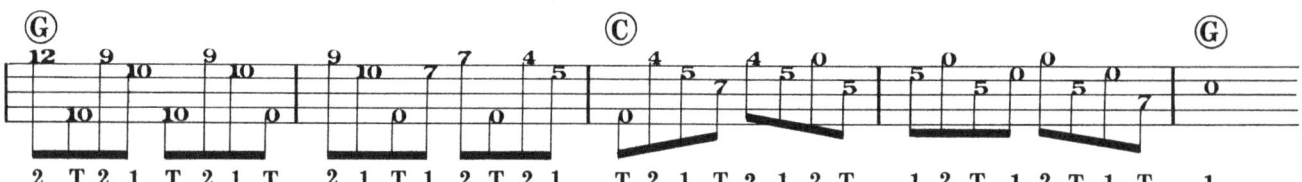

You can use this in the first four measures of a tune like "Foggy Mountain Breakdown," or in the beginning of a song that has its first two measures in G and the second two in C, as indicated above. When you divide this run into sections, it can also have several other applications. For instance, you can start with the fifth note of the second measure and take it through to the fourth note of the fourth measure to produce a lick which will go nicely with a two bar D chord:

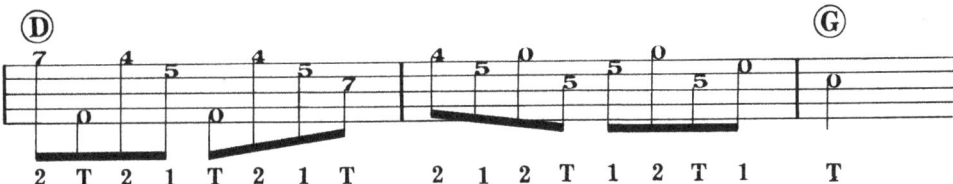

You can explore other possibilities on your own.

Ascending runs also fit nicely into this style. Here's an almost infinite one that Bobby plays on "Foxfire":

In the midst of all these melodic runs, you should realize that Bobby is also a fine Scruggs player. His break to "Are You Missing Me" features his own driving and syncopated approach, coupled with a dash of tasteful melodics. By looking at the sixth and seventh bars, you can see how he gets the syncopation:

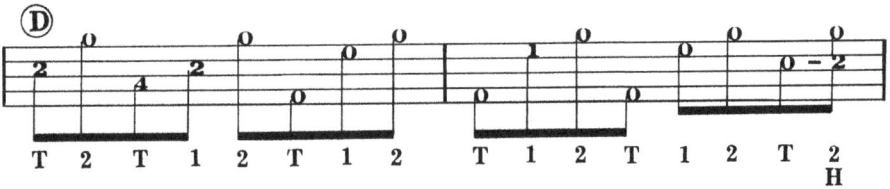

The important thing to notice is that he's playing four forward rolls in a row. These forward rolls repeat every three notes (T12, T12, and so on), and since the standard 2/4 measure has the beat falling once every four notes, the beginning of the forward roll and the downbeat will only coincide once every twelve notes. At all other times the thumb will pick the string at various places in between downbeats and syncopation will result.

One other interesting thing about his break is the melodic lick found in the last D chord:

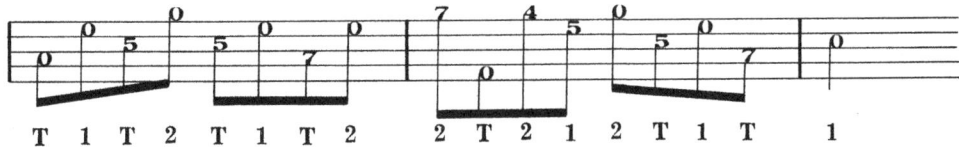

It's close to, but not the same as, Bill Keith's "Noah Crase Lick."

By comparing these two licks you can get some insight into the stylistic differences between Keith and Thompson. Bobby's version is bouncier and involves more left hand movement, while Bill's is more self-contained, being based on one left hand position. In many ways these characteristics hold true on a larger scale if you consider the general scope of their individual styles.

This final example is an exercise to demonstrate how some of the runs mentioned earlier can be applied to a simple three chord progression. I've taken several of Bobby's licks and strung them end to end for this purpose:

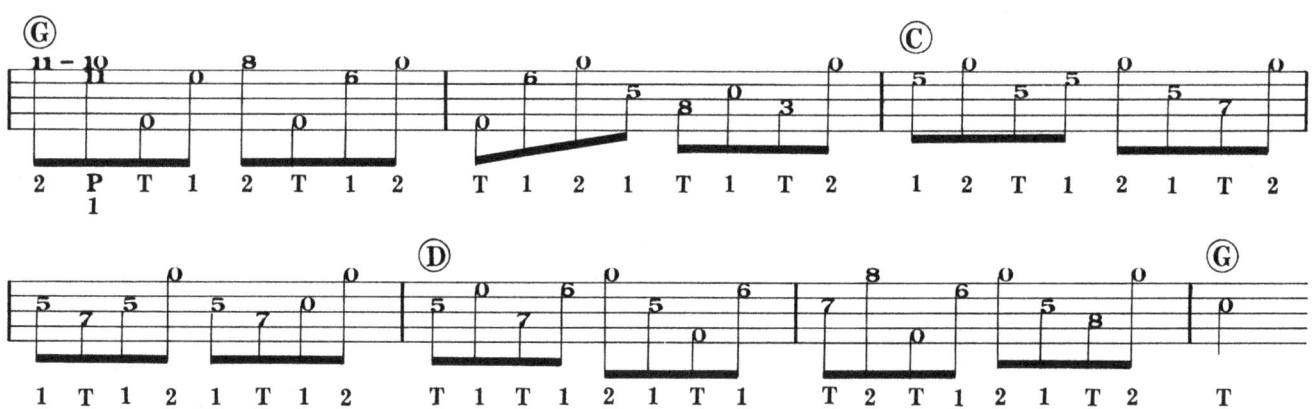

I want to stress that this *is* only an exercise, because judged as a piece of music it makes excessive use of these runs. As you learn more "fancy" licks you may be tempted to recklessly throw them into songs. The trick, though, is not to overdo it. A piece of music needs periods of simplicity to contrast with the more complex sections. Bobby's style, in the following tablature, is a model of balance and good taste as far as this is concerned. To quote Bobby, "I've gotten to where I kind of play with whatever mood I'm in instead of getting so technical about it. I'd rather play a simple lick and put a little feeling in it than play 10,000 notes with no feel. Music is a kind of expression of your feelings and when you start getting too technical it loses that."

# Katy Hill

Traditional
Bobby Thompson
Arranged and adapted by Area Code 615

Key of G
Part A

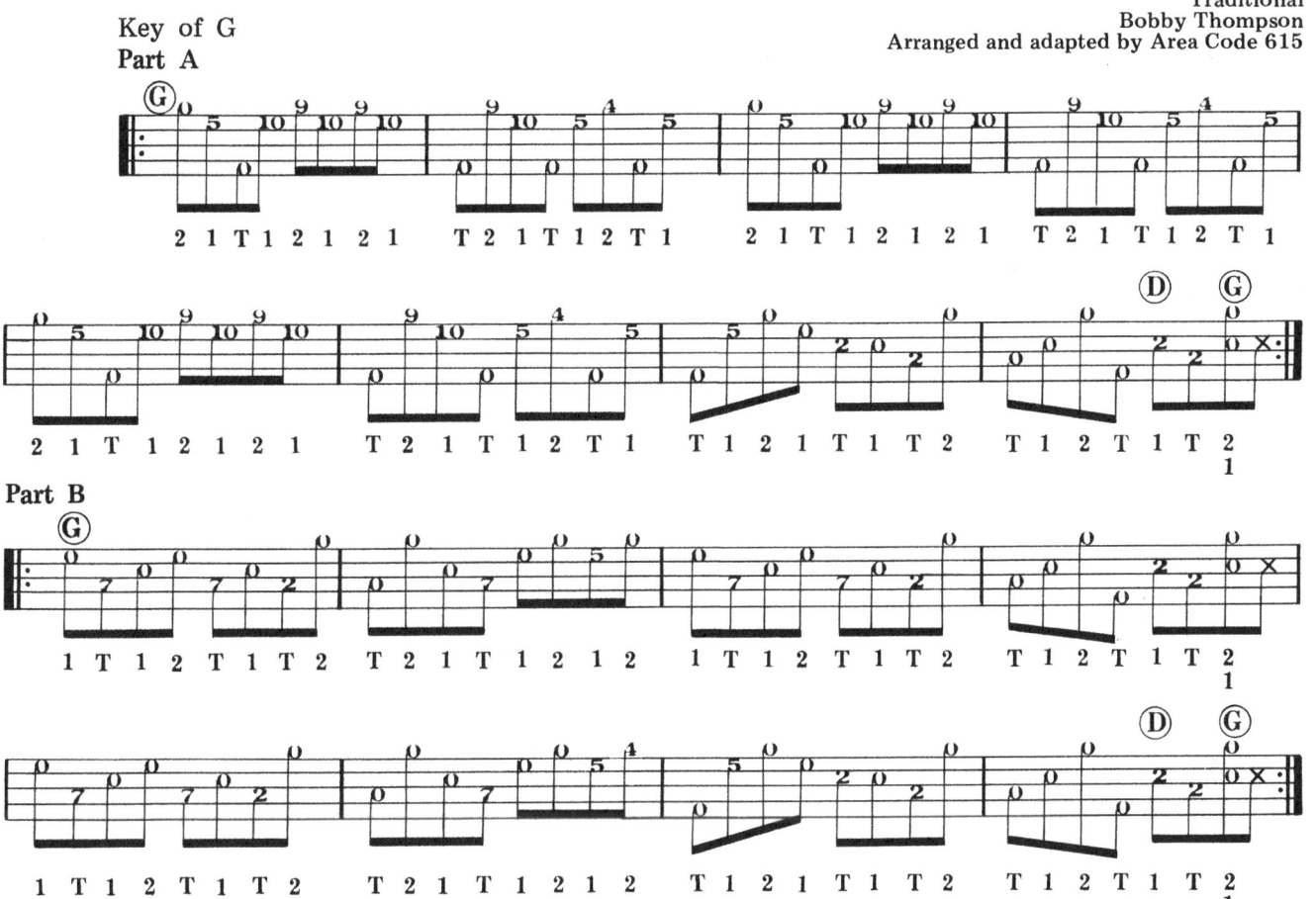

© 615 Music. All Rights Reserved. Used by Permission.

As played on Area Code 615 *Trip in the Country*, Polydor Records 24-4025

# Are You Missing Me

Ira and Charles Louvin

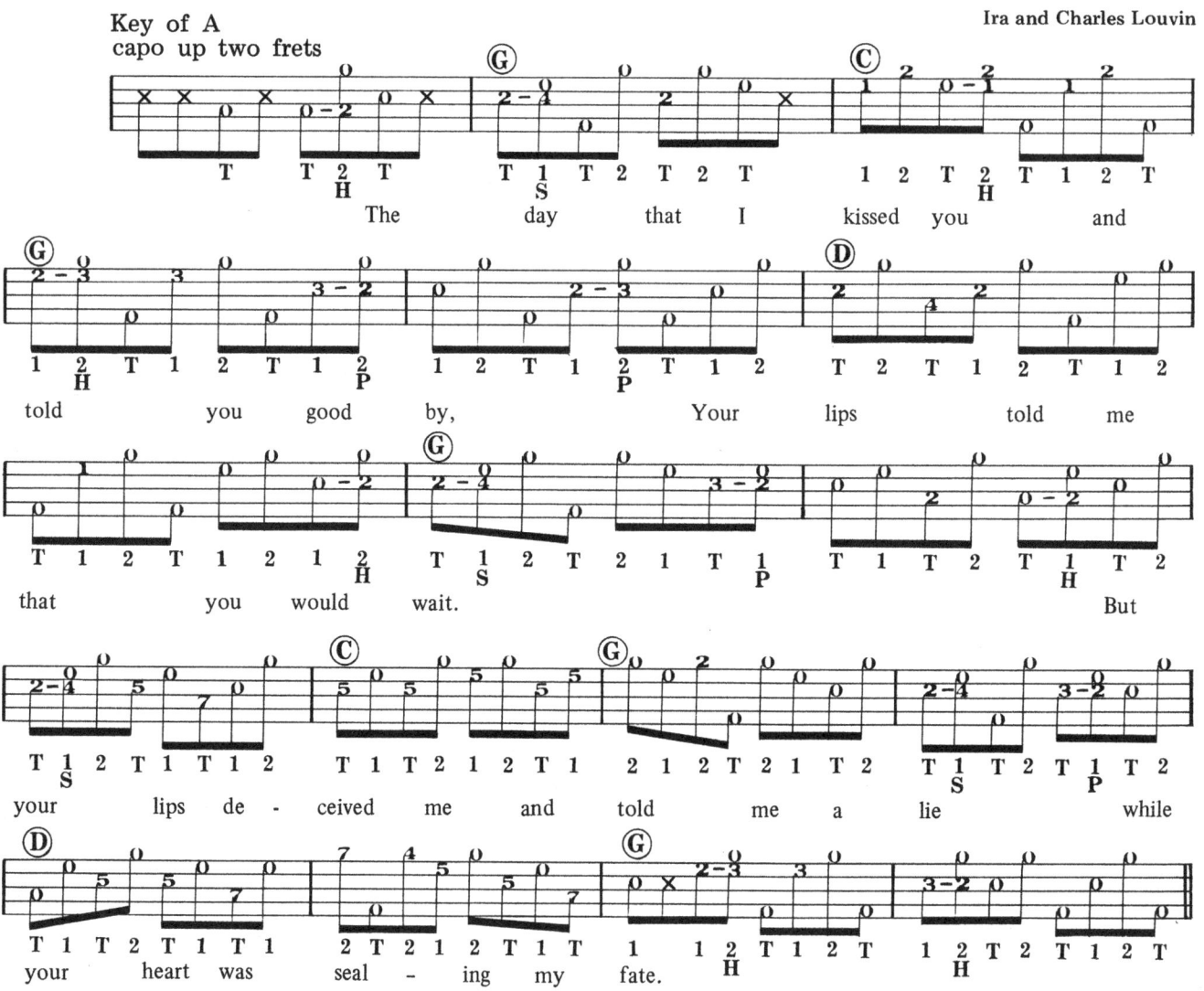

© Copyright 1952 by Acuff-Rose Publications, Inc. Used by Permission of the Publisher. All Rights Reserved.

From a live tape of *Jim and Jesse* at the 1966 Roanoke Bluegrass Festival

## "DEVIL DANCE" AND "FOXFIRE"

In some ways, these two songs are the most advanced ones in this book. In terms of setting, overall structure, and rhythmic conception, they cover exciting new territory for the banjo.

"Devil Dance" was recorded with just banjo and percussion, which immediately takes it out of the bluegrass realm. Instead of using a standard "boom-chink" bluegrass feel, the drums rhythmically echo the syncopated blues notes that Bobby plays; and for once you find yourself listening to the banjo as more of a rhythm instrument than a melodic one.

If you look at the introduction, you can see how Bobby has adapted to the new setting. He breaks away from the mandatory stream of sixteenth notes common to most banjo breaks by leaving five note rests at the end of every two bars. Spaces like this are unheard of in bluegrass, and in a sense, he's teaching us to look at the banjo in a whole new light.

"Foxfire" is equally impressive, though for different reasons. It's a highly melodic tune, and though you've heard some of the runs before, Bobby combines them in new and interesting ways. In addition, he plays with a lot of rhythmic subtlety, especially in the last four bars of Part A. What's more striking, however, is the structure of the tune. The first time through he plays three complete, related sections, adding a fourth part the second time around. Since most bluegrass tunes only have two parts—with the exception of a few like "Dusty Miller" and "Gray Eagle"—"Foxfire" represents an expanded musical conception. Of course, in this case also, the setting isn't strictly bluegrass. There's a string section, female chorus and set of drums that back him up. But if you can get past that, you'll hear some of the most solid and inventive banjo playing on record.

# Devil Dance

Key of G

Bobby Thompson and Kenny Malone

© Sandstorm Music, Inc., 1974. All Rights Reserved. Used by Permission.

From Capricorn Records CPR-0076

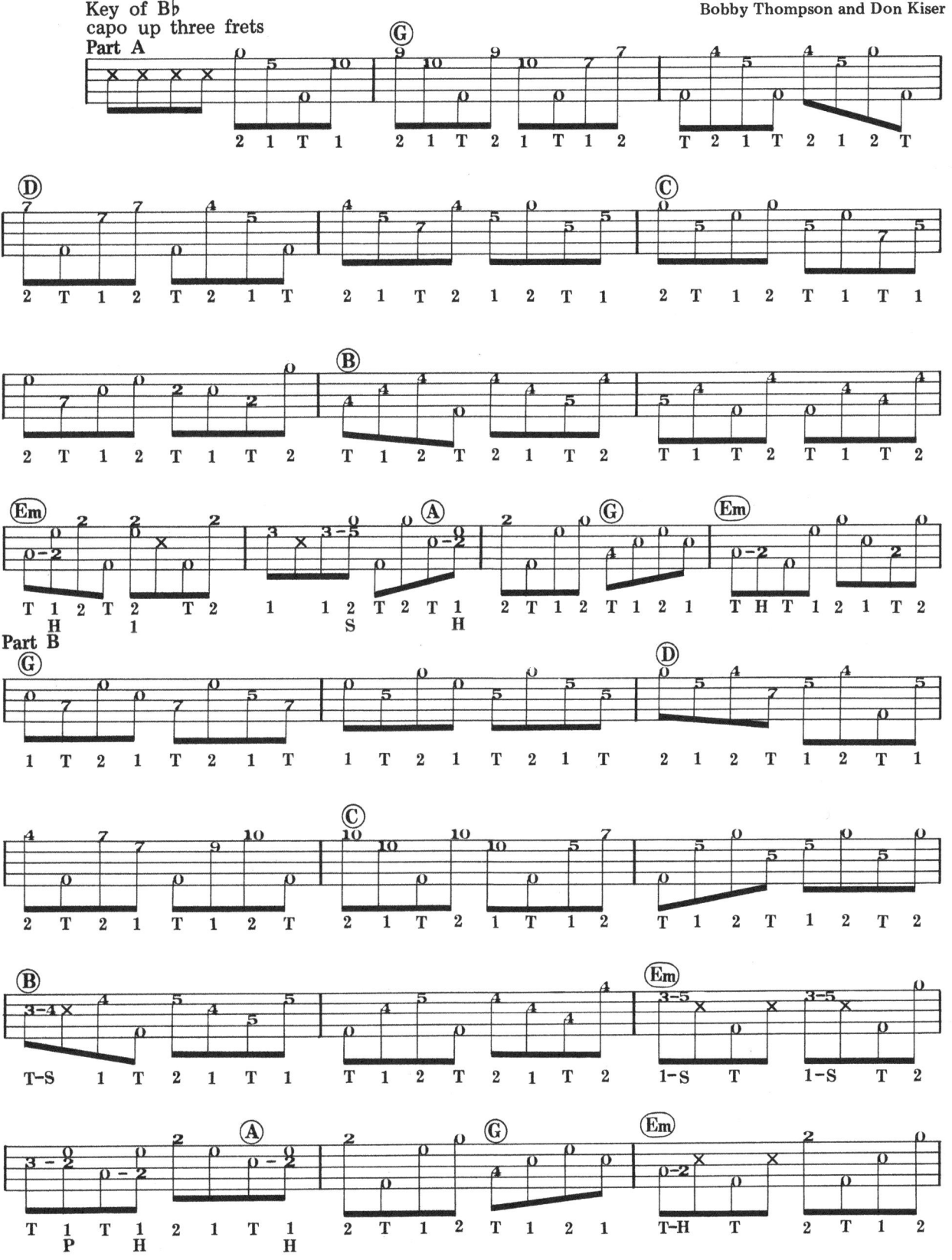

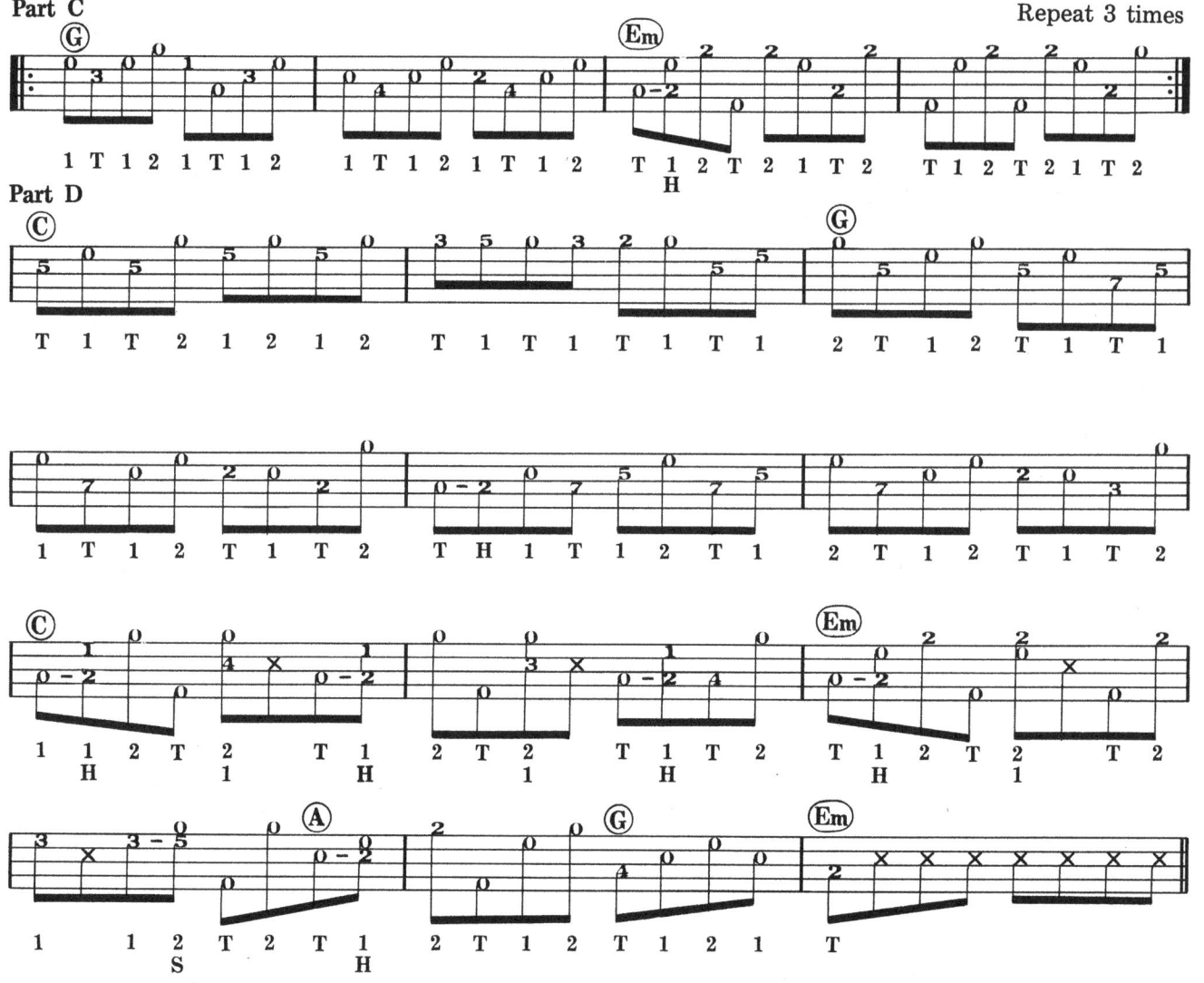

From Capricorn Records CPR-0076

## INTERVIEW WITH BOBBY THOMPSON

Tony: When did you start playing banjo?
Bobby: It was probably '51 or '52.
T: What first interested you in playing?
B: A friend of mine started playing guitar and I heard "Foggy Mountain Breakdown." I didn't even know what the instrument was, but I found out and I decided I'd try that.
T: Did you have any lessons?
B: No I just picked it up, most of it from records.
T: Who did you listen to back then besides Scruggs? Did you listen to Don Reno?
B: Yeah. Those were the only two I knew of that played.
T: What was your first professional job?
B: I worked with two or three groups, but playing with Carl Story was the first really professional job I had.
T: What songs did you record with him?
B: There was "Banjolina," "Fire on the Banjo," and a couple of gospel things that I can't remember. I just did one session with him ... four tunes. I believe Tommy Jackson played fiddle on them. That was '57 or '58.
T: Was it right around this time that you began working on your melodic style?
B: Yeah. Benny Sims (a fiddler) made the suggestion. We used to work a lot of double shows together with Carl Story and *Bonny Lou and Buster* out of Johnson City, Tennessee. Benny was working with them. He kind of gave me the idea to see the banjo play note-for-note like a fiddle tune. So I sat down and started fiddling with it.
T: Did he suggest any specific tunes to you?
B: No. He just gave me the idea and I worked on it myself. The first tune I worked out was "Arkansas Traveler."
T: After that you went to work with *Jim and Jesse*?
B: Right. It must have been sometime in '58 when I went with them and I guess I stayed with them until '60. The first time I worked with Jesse, no matter what time we got to bed he was up at seven o'clock in the morning, and he'd always write a tune, every morning. He'd get me and Vassar Clements, and we'd just sit around and work it up. Next day was a different tune. . . . and now, I'd give anything for just part of those tunes we did. We never got the rest of the band to learn any of them—the next day there'd be another one. Just having fun. Then I went in the army. Only playing I did was this one sergeant had this one tune, "San Antonio Rose," and when he got drunk, and I'd play that tune, I got out of all details for the next week.[4]
When I came out, I played bass with a group for about six months and then I decided I was going to quit it, and threw it all on the bed and didn't touch it for two or three years. I just worked in a machine shop. Then the bug got me again. In '64 or '65 I picked up the banjo again and played lead guitar a little bit. I was just jamming with local guys. Then *Jim and Jesse* got me to go back with them, so I moved to Nashville. I stayed on the road for a year or so with them, then got tired of the road again and quit. I finally worked into doing a few sessions. Then I found out I was going to starve if I didn't play something besides banjo. So I picked up guitar and got into some rhythm work.

---

[4] Quote courtesy of *Bluegrass Unlimited*.

Bobby Thompson with *Jim and Jesse* and Vassar Clements.

T: What kind of music were you listening to back then?
B: I used to listen to a little bit of everything. I used to listen to a lot of jazz, then I just completely lost interest in it.
T: When did you first hear Bill Keith?
B: I can't remember the first time I heard Bill play.... maybe it was on the Opry. The first tune I heard him play was "Sailor's Hornpipe," and I thought it was great.
T: How did you come to meet him?
B: A friend of mine, Don Limeburger, was working with Bill Monroe at one time, and he first told me about Keith, and I'd never heard him play. So then Bill called me one day, and I wasn't even knowing who he was, because I wasn't really keeping up with it back then. I had just picked the banjo back up and started messing with it again. So he came down and we just sat around and picked awhile. Bill went farther with the melodic style than I had, 'cause I'd kind of stalled out and pretty much forgotten about it. I know there was two years there where I didn't much touch it. I know everybody always asks me this, and I really don't have no good answer. I don't know if he got anything from me or if he just run up on it same as I did.
T: How about those descending blues runs and scales?
B: I got hung up on that for a few years and never got to use it 'til we did *Area Code 615*. I guess that was the period I was really into it.
T: Those runs involved taking guitar licks and applying them to the banjo?
B: Well, you'd hear a run that maybe you couldn't do on banjo, but you could work something around it. I kind of got into the habit of hearing a lick enough to halfway remember it, then sitting down and coming up with something around it so I wouldn't be doing the same thing. I picked that up from a lot of the studio guys I was working with.
T: You like working in the studio?
B: Yeah, I really do. The money's good. I'd say that. There's always variety. Working with a regular band you've usually got a show worked up. You do the same tunes night after night, and you might change one or two songs and that's about it. In the studio, you never know what you're going to do until you get there. When I go in I don't know if I'm playing guitar, banjo, or what. It really keeps it interesting. You have to be constantly coming up with new things to keep working, and you're always around new ideas. That's what I enjoy about it.
T: Who have you listened to and learned from in the Nashville studios?
B: A lot of people. I guess Wayne Moss, Grady Martin, Charlie McCoy—I got a lot of blues stuff from Charlie. And a lot of the steel players—Lloyd Green, Hal Rugg, Weldon Myrick.
T: What else have you learned in the studio?
B: You've got to cut commercial records, and then when you kind of get off the track, they calm you down and you begin to realize that you're selling to the public, not musicians.

**T:** Getting back to the melodic style, what would you suggest to someone who's just getting into it?

**B:** I think if you're going to learn banjo you should learn the basic Scruggs and Reno style along with the other, because there are so many types of music where that's all you need, basic licks fit best. With melodic stuff there's no set rolls or patterns, you just have to figure out a way you can get the notes and adapt the roll to get it. And that gets pretty confusing on some of the fiddle tunes. You'll go through them and there may be five notes different. You have to remember which one you're playing. That happens to me. I'll get two or three tunes confused. I'll get into it and then realize I'm going the wrong way and try to get out of it and can't. I think it's a style you have to play enough to do without thinking about it.

Bobby Thompson

# Chromatic Runs

Some people use the term *chromatic* to describe the overall melodic style. This, actually, is a misnomer. *Chromatic* is a very specific term which simply refers to two or more consecutive notes which are a half step apart from each other. Take this series of notes for example:

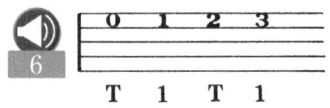 This can be more easily done melodically: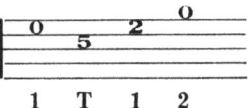

Here's an extension of this idea which covers a whole octave:

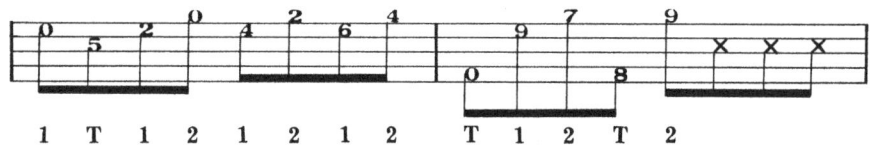

(The A part of my break to "Paddy on the Turnpike" on the insert record contains about half of this run.)

Most people prefer to use chromatics on a limited basis, because in large doses they can be pretty exhausting on the ear. Alan Munde integrates them tastefully into his break for "Lonesome Blues," and Courtney Johnson does the same in "Cold Sailor." Here's a chromatic lick that I use from time to time.

Not every interval here is chromatic, but enough are to give the lick that feel. This run works nicely at the beginning of "Foggy Mountain Breakdown" or "Lonesome Road Blues."

The main characteristic of chromatics is that of ambiguity. Since a long chromatic run can involve every note in an octave, the only thing that aligns it with a particular key is the note that it starts with and the one that it ends on. This means that once you get the hang of this business you can create runs out of thin air. Just pick your first and last notes so that they fit with the chord that you're playing over, and fill in the center with chromatics. For instance, here's a chromatic lick for the key of C that I made up while I was writing this paragraph:

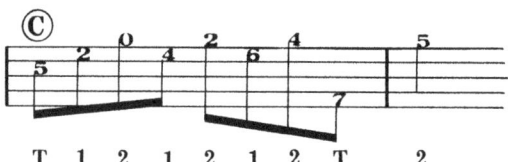

Since there are so few licks in this idiom, it's up to you to work up some more.

# Eric Weissberg
# and Marshall Brickman

Eric Weissberg lives in the recording studios of New York City. Whenever a session comes in for banjo, guitar, pedal steel, mandolin, bass, dobro or fiddle, he's the one to get first call. Of these instruments, of course he's best known for his banjo work. After all, he's been playing the banjo longer than most people on the bluegrass scene today, and over the years he's had a strong effect on many pickers.

In the early 60s he and Marshall Brickman got together to make two influential records, *Folk Banjo Styles* and *New Dimensions in Bluegrass* (recently repackaged as the *Soundtrack from Deliverance*). *Folk Banjo Styles* featured some of the earliest examples of melodic playing to be found anywhere, including one of the few recorded examples of note-for-note double banjo melodic playing (on "Devil's Dream"). The *New Dimensions* album was even more revolutionary in that it contained several songs with shocking (for bluegrass) chord changes, plus experimental arrangements of more familiar tunes, such as "Farewell Blues." The fact that Eric went to Juilliard may account for some of this radical behavior.

In short, both albums were responsible for opening up new possibilities of expression on the banjo, and for spreading the gospel of the melodic style to a mass audience.

On these records Eric comes across as being stylistically more conservative than Marshall. Although he's fluent in the melodic style he prefers a more Scruggs-oriented approach. . . . "I like to play really strong, with not too much going on." The melodic work that he does is fairly down to earth, and except in the full-length treatment of instrumentals such as "Eighth of January," he uses it only sparingly. "I still like to do little snatches of it. But I don't enjoy the really long runs that seem to be in vogue now." To demonstrate here's part of the chorus of "Old Joe Clark" played in Eric's style. (Notice the melodic blues lick in the last measure—a harbinger of things to come.)

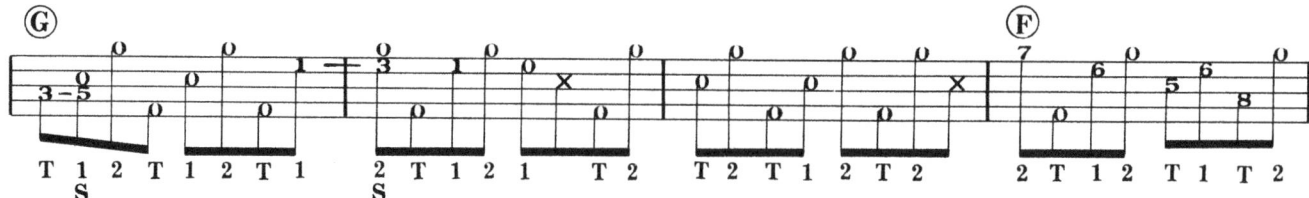

Marshall Brickman was influenced by Eric Weissberg and Bill Keith, but took their styles off into a more experimental direction. He was way ahead of his time in the early 60s, and even today his playing from back then sounds futuristic by bluegrass standards.

The break he takes on "Shuckin' the Corn" is a good example of his style, featuring long Keith-like runs, combined with chromatic notes and jazz-like phrasing. For the chromatics, look at measures 5 through 8 of his second break:

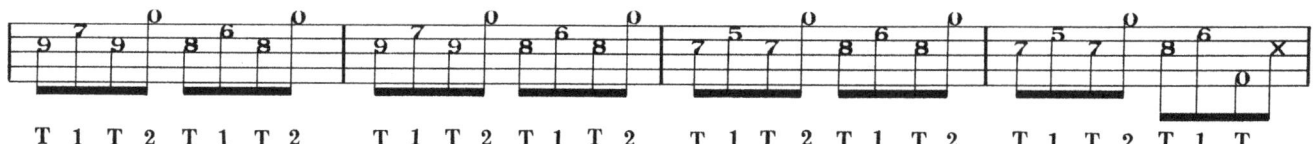

This sounds complicated, but it's actually very easy to play. He's just taking a simple left hand finger position,

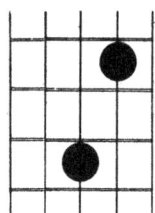

and moving it up and down three frets, one fret at a time. Since the notes on each succeeding fret are a half step apart, this is how he gets the chromatic sound.

As for his unusual phrasing, look at the last two bars of his first break and the first two bars of his second break:

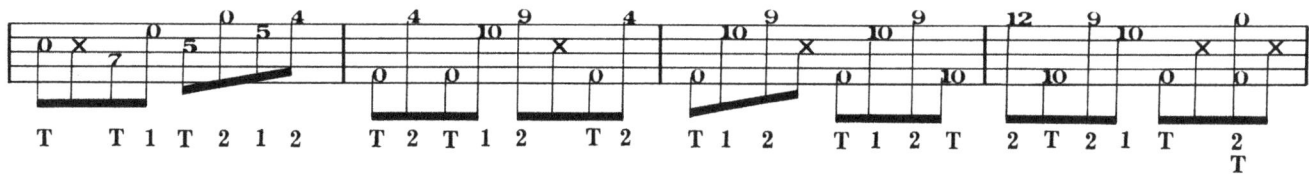

For these four bars Marshall is taking a simple ascending line,

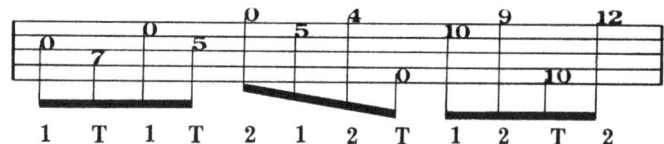

and dissecting it, arranging the resulting phrases so that they begin and end in unexpected places. For instance, look at the middle two of the four measures mentioned above:

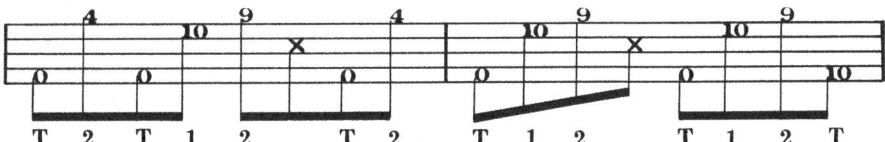

Notice that the first five notes and the second five notes are exactly the same. The only difference is that the first five start on the downbeat while the second five begin on the offbeat. It's little tricks like this that make his phrasing so exciting.

Before we get into the tablature for this chapter, let me mention that "Devil's Dream" features Eric and Marshall alternating verses and choruses. This gives you a good chance to compare their styles side by side, Eric taking the first halves of the A and B parts, and Marshall the second halves.

# Devil's Dream

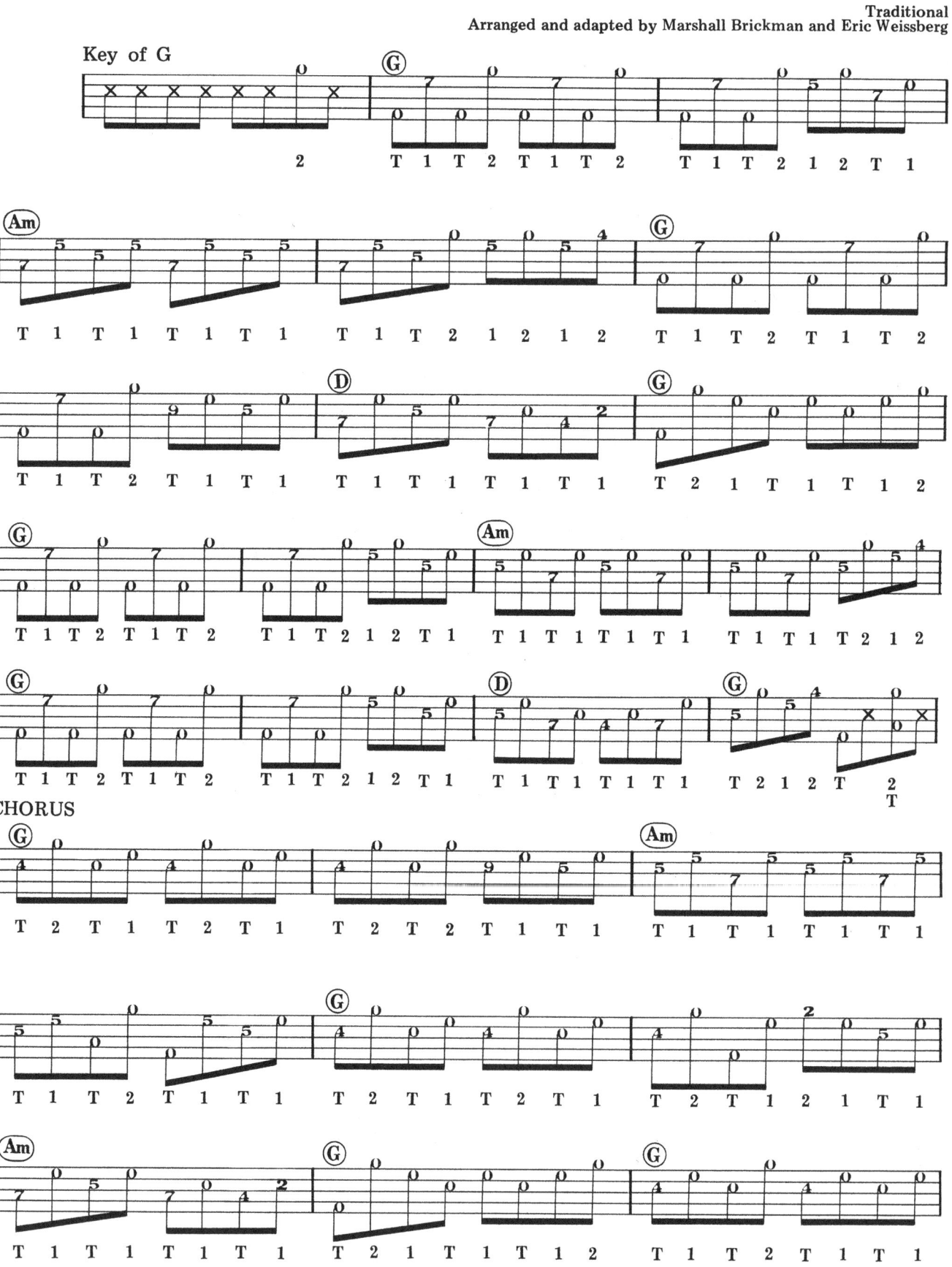

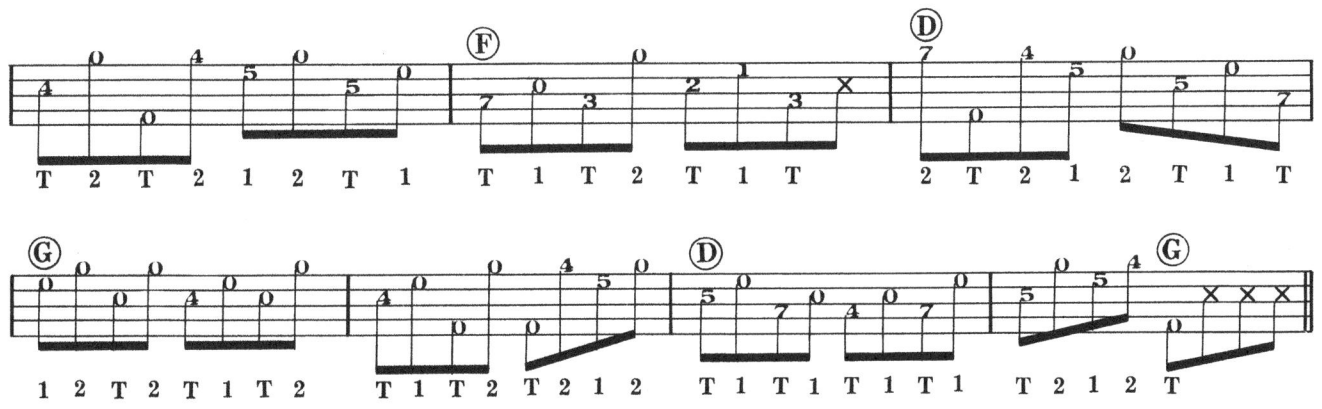

From *Folk Banjo Styles*, Elektra Records EKL-217

# Eighth Of January

Traditional
Arranged and adapted by Marshall Brickman and Eric Weissberg

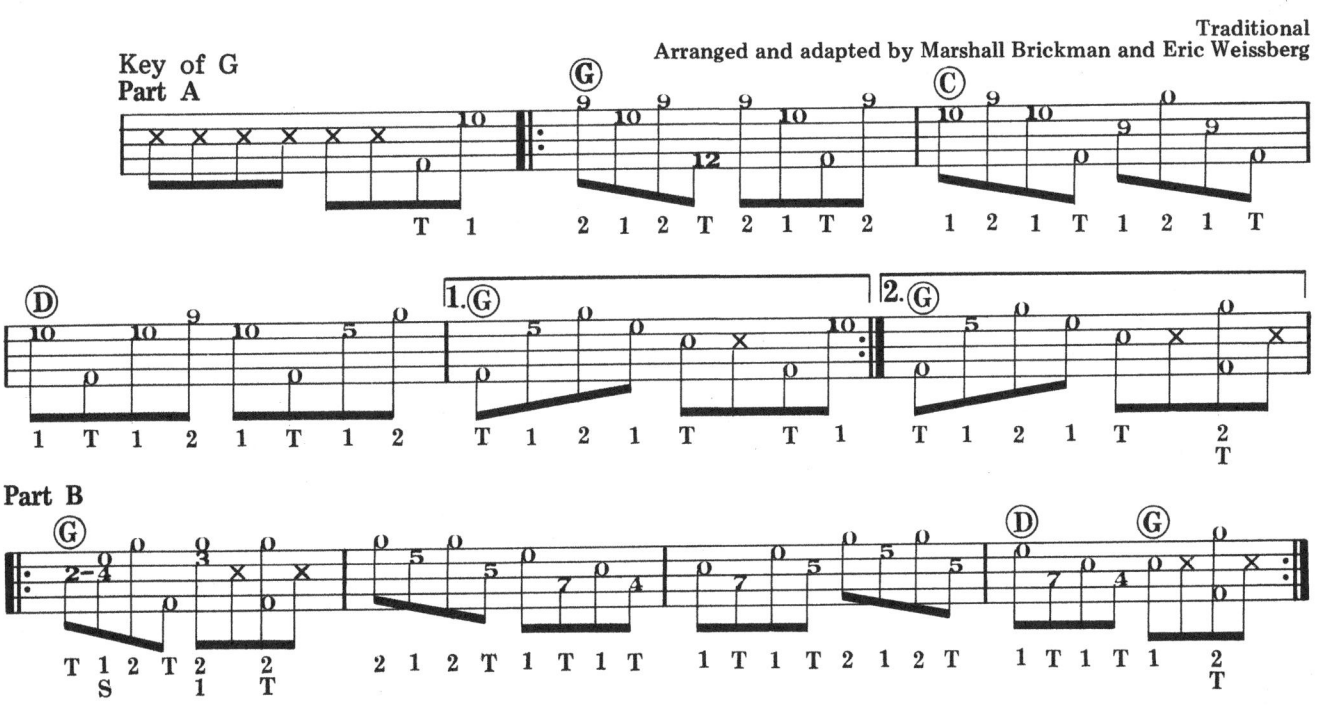

© 1973 Warner-Tamerlane Publishing Corporation. All Rights Reserved. Used by Permission.

From *Deliverance*, Warner Brothers Records BS-2683

# Fire On The Mountain

Traditional
Arranged and adapted by Marshall Brickman and Eric Weissberg

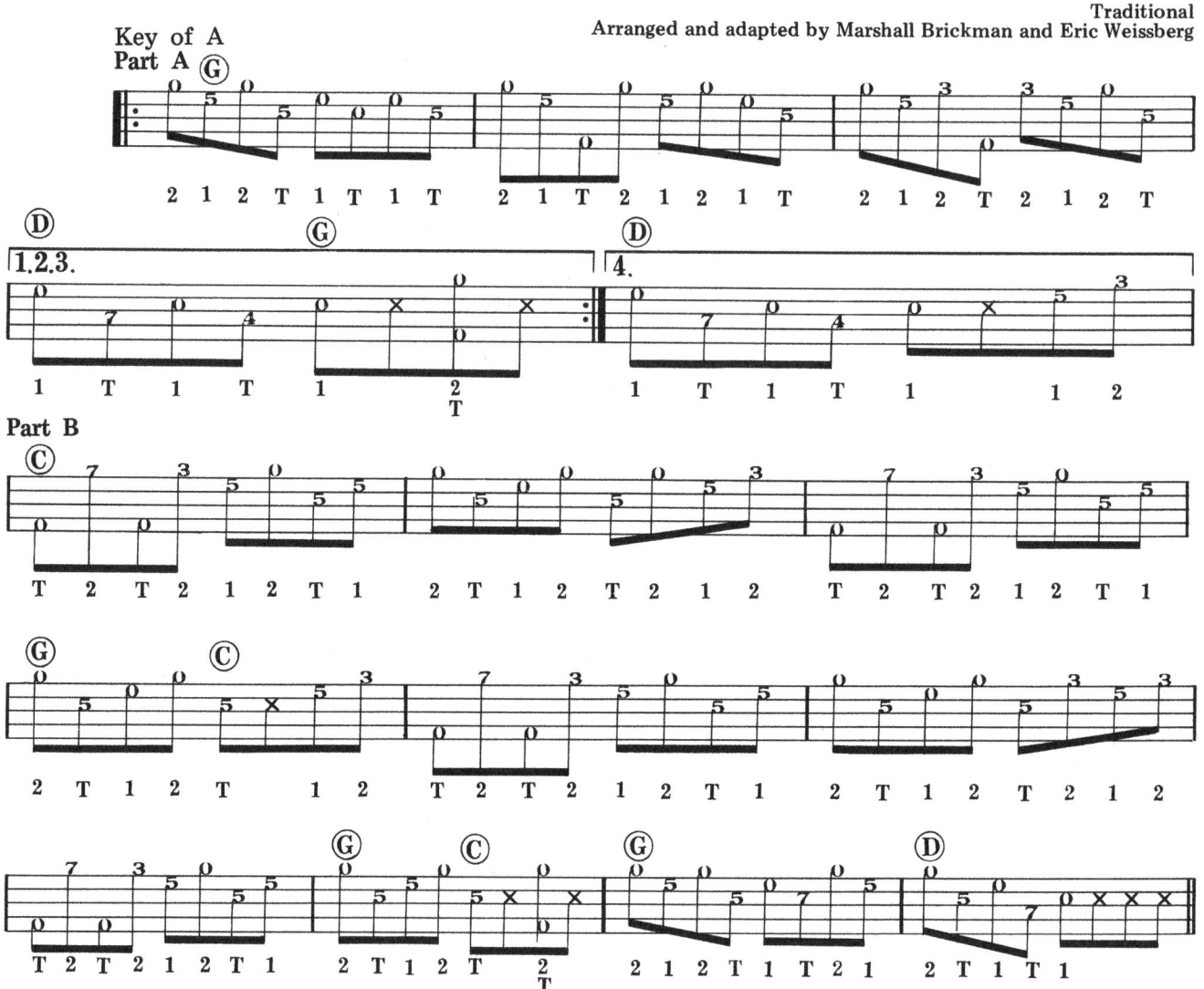

© 1973 Warner-Tamerlane Publishing Corporation. All Rights Reserved. Used by Permission.

From *Deliverance*, Warner Brothers Records BS-2683

# Shuckin' The Corn

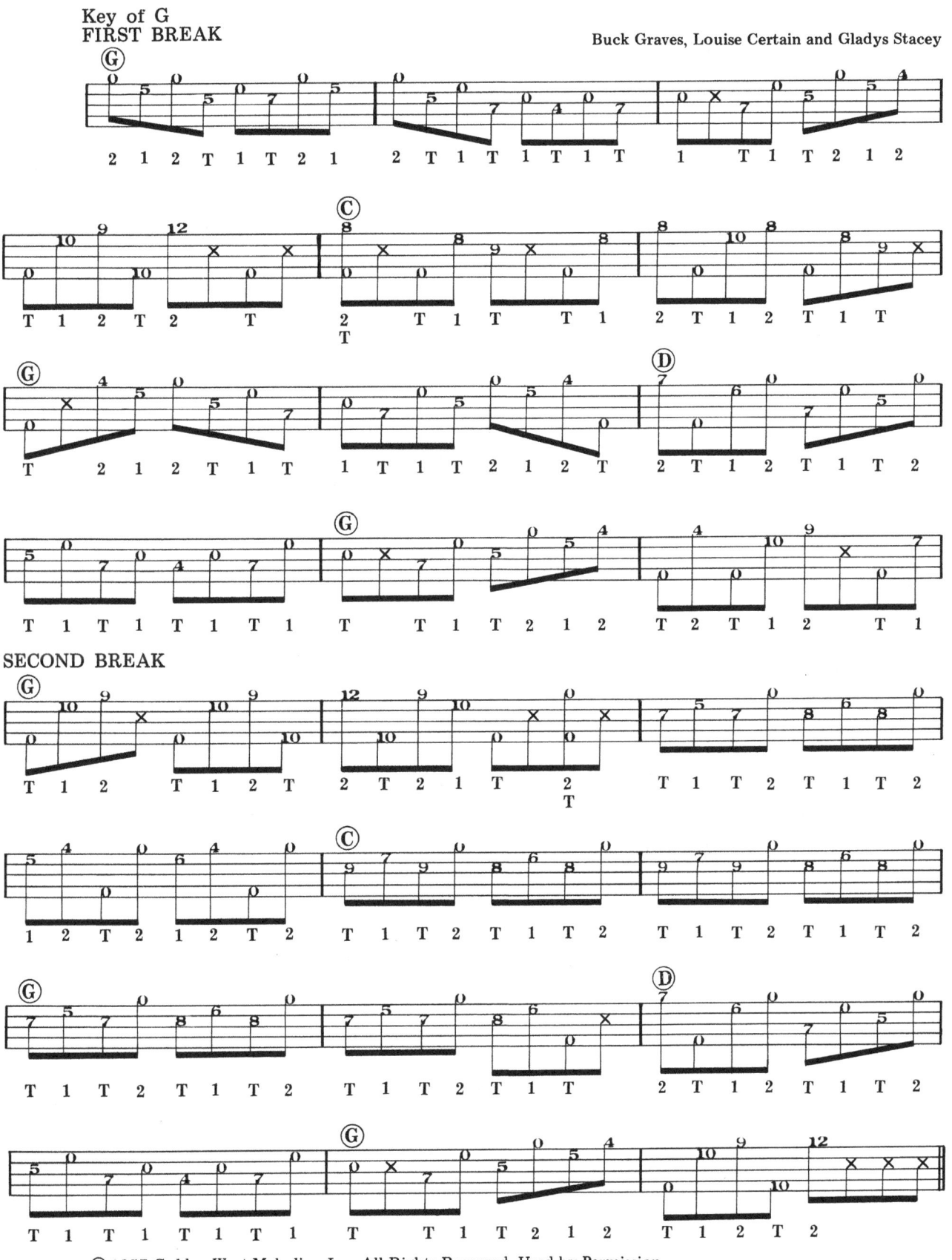

© 1957 Golden West Melodies, Inc. All Rights Reserved. Used by Permission.

From *Deliverance*, Warner Brothers Records BS-2683

# INTERVIEW WITH ERIC WEISSBERG

Tony: How did you first get interested in banjo?

Eric: Pete Seeger. I started around 1947 or '48. I had a friend who was studying guitar and banjo and whenever he came over he would show me a couple of things. And I went to a camp where Pete (Seeger) was a guest and I used to watch him. In those days, it was relatively simple. It was just frailing, not picking the stuff. There wasn't too much happening. So I played that style until I was twelve or thirteen. I was in junior high school and I was playing fiddle in an assembly program for a square dance. The guy behind me was playing the banjo. He was three or four years older than I, and his name was Mike Steig, son of the cartoonist Steig, and he was playing three-finger style I'd never heard before. It was all I could do to play fiddle. I couldn't believe what was going on. He was playing on a riser and the banjo was even with my ear. I tried to get him to show me what he was doing and he just wouldn't show me anything. And how I got the first rudiments was his girlfriend, Dina, showed me: 1 2 T 1 2 T 1 2, you know. So I went home and I'm sure I drove my parents crazy for the next five years. A little after that I discovered a place to get *Flatt and Scruggs* records and an occasional Don Reno record. This was '50 or '51. It was a little place on 4th Avenue and 14th Street called *Berliners*. A little card shop and record shop. Very tiny. But he had a couple of playbooths. And I used to go in Monday and Friday, after school to see if he got any new records in. The first Scruggs record I bought was "I'll Stay Around." I brought that home and put it on the phonograph and I said to myself, "There's no way that guy is playing all those notes."

T: How did you know to listen to Scruggs? Who turned you on to Scruggs?

E: Dina or Mike said, "Well, it's Scruggs style." It's a weird word, Scruggs. I thought it was some kind of generic term or some kind of mechanical or chemical term. I guess I was playing in Washington Square then. I started in the late '40s on Sundays. So maybe I heard the term bandied about there. I just began to play more and more. There was no thumb lead, it was all first finger lead because I couldn't figure out what he was doing. With 78s it was really hard because I'd slow them down to 33 and I'd have to change key. I used to sit in front of the phonograph for hours. That's how I taught myself the style. I guess there was a breakthrough somewhere. Time went on and I guess the first Newport Folk Festival was in 1959 and I was playing bass with Leon Bibb. Bill Keith tells me this story. Those early festivals, at night you'd go down to the beach and sit around the fire and play. Bill tells me I was the first guy he really heard play five-string banjo close up. He heard me play and then he got into it. I think I was the first guy that a lot of people heard really play that style. Marshall Brickman tells me I was the first person he heard play that style also. That was when we were about fifteen; we were at a party, or somebody's Bar Mitzvah or something like that.

T: How did you meet Marshall?

E: I didn't really know him. We had mutual friends. He went to a different camp. We were both from New York. I met him and we both dug each other right away and he was interested in the banjo also. To get back to Bill, in the early '60s I was starting to experiment very slowly with semi-melodic stuff. I wasn't playing full tunes melodically, but I was doing little riffs that had that kind of style in them.

T: Did you do this out of your own head?

E: Yeah, it was in my head. There was a little section of something I wanted to play note-for-note so I had to figure it out. But it was very restricted. I don't think it was more than sixteen notes at a time, then you go back into the other thing. Then around 1960 or '61 I met Bill at a friend's house. Bill, by this time, was really working on his own style. Marshall and I went over and Billy started playing some of this. The first thing he played was "Salty Dog." It was another staggering thing. He did it melodically and it was a mindblower. It inspired me and Marshall. But I certainly have to give credit to Bill for really going through with it all the way. It's funny how things can happen in different parts of the country at the same time. I'll never forget, I was doing a sort of tenor style, single string stuff, alternating thumb and first finger, playing melody that way. And Reno was doing the same thing at the same time. And he came out with a record at just about the same time I was really getting into it. I think it was "Follow the Leader." So we were both doing that simultaneously. This was the very late '50s. I was doing it myself and then I heard him doing it and I said, "Wow, that's really weird." Marshall really flipped out for Bill's style more than I did. I mean I loved listening to it, and I loved working it out to a point, and I love listening to Bill play, he's great. And I enjoyed it while I was doing it. Of course Marshall and I worked up a lot of it in thirds. I don't think it had ever been done before really. We did it on "Devil's Dream." Two people doing the melodic stuff note-for-note. Then when Marshall and I did the *New Dimensions* album, I guess I was a little more into it. And I did a couple of things on it that were pretty much the whole style. I found it rewarding, but I found it very taxing to do that. There's so much concentration and memory work. There's something about it that doesn't have the drive for me. I'd almost rather listen to Earl than anybody. It's so right.

I was going to Juilliard, 1959, at the time and I was studying to be a classical bassist.

T: What about Marshall?

E: He ended up going to Wisconsin and he was about to go to Juilliard as a composition major.

T: Did he play anything besides banjo?

E: He played piano and accordion, which he'll never admit, and a little trumpet.

T: What was the story behind "Dueling Banjos?"

E: It was a call. They said, "Do you know 'Dueling Banjos'?" and I said, "Well, yeah." And they said, "Well, we've got this movie." So I got Steve (Mandel) and we went down there, rehearsed with the director, and he told us how he wanted to shoot the scene. And then we went into the studio and recorded it twenty times at slightly different time lengths. He liked it so much, he wanted us to do the rest of the sound track. So we went back down the next weekend; this was in Atlanta. And we played "Dueling Banjos" until it was coming out our ears.

T: How did it get to be a hit?

E: It was Boorman, the director. He said, "This is going to be a hit record." They put it out as a promotional thing to play behind the D. J. announcing the movie. And people began to call in about it. "Is that a record or what?" And it got back to Warner Brothers and they decided to release it as an official record. Who would have expected to make that much money off a session?

Eric Weissberg, Arthur Fiedler, Earl Robinson and Pete Seeger. Before the performance of Earl Robinson's *Banjo Concerto*, Boston Symphony Hall, 1967.

# Second Generation Melodic Players

This section will touch on six modern players who have helped to spread the popularity of the melodic style, both on records and in live appearances. The one thing they have in common is the fact that they've all learned from either Bill Keith or Bobby Thompson and have since gone on to make their own unique contributions.

Of course, there are many other fine musicians who fit into this category, such as Pat Cloud, Butch Robbins, Bob Black, Larry McNeely, Jimmy Arnold, Garland Shuping and Pete Schwimmer, but the list is too long and space too short, so I've focused on these six as being the most representative.

**BEN ELDRIDGE**

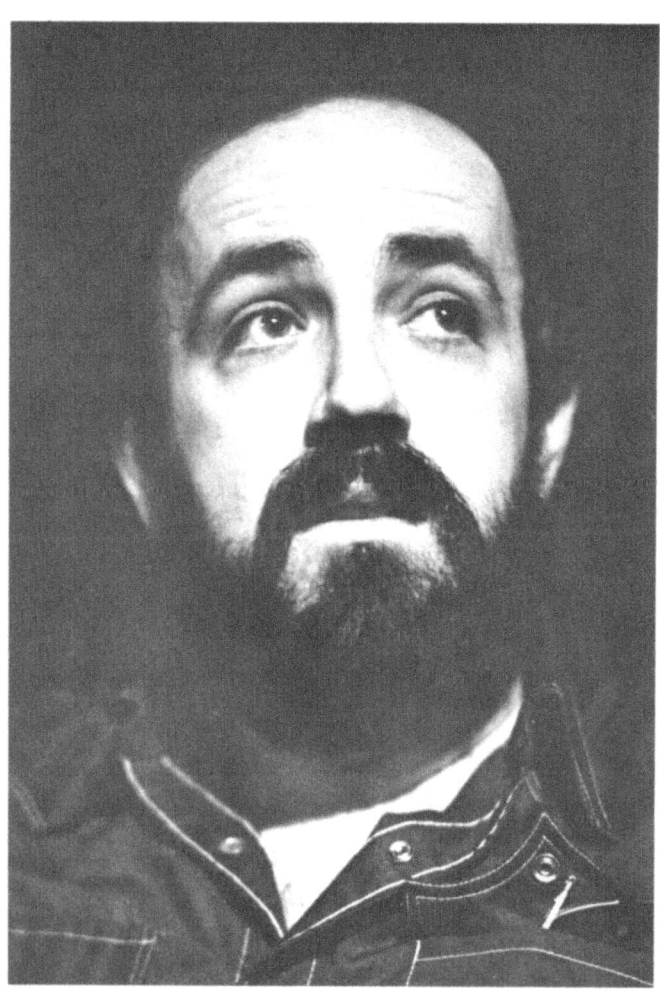

A successful mathematician, Ben Eldridge is also known for his work on the banjo. In fact, he's considered by many to be one of the best all-around banjo players in bluegrass. On recordings with Mike Auldridge, Cliff Waldron and the *Seldom Scene*, his drive and sense of good taste always shine through.

As a boy, his first musical inclination was toward accordion, but his parents couldn't afford one and instead bought him a $13 Sears and Roebuck guitar. A couple of years later, at age fifteen, he heard *Flatt and Scruggs* on the radio playing "Foggy Mountain Breakdown" and "I'll Just Pretend:" "I heard something going on in the backup and I didn't know what the heck it was, but I thought it was really neat." He talked his father into buying him a banjo for his sixteenth birthday, and a friend showed him how to tune it, and play a few rolls. "I just started playing *Flatt and Scruggs* records. Scruggs and Don Reno were the first guys I ever listened to. That was in 1954. I grew up in Richmond, Virginia, and *Flatt and Scruggs* were on the Old Dominion Barndance and I used to watch them on their live radio shows from 11:30 to 12:00. Scruggs was absolutely amazing back them." He spent the next years mastering Scruggs style, but in 1957 took four years off from playing banjo to go to college.

Then in 1963 he heard Bill Keith for the first time: "I heard Keith at a park show when he was with Bill Monroe, and heard him play 'Devil's Dream' and just absolutely couldn't believe my ears. It was amazing." Fortunately, a friend of Ben's taped the show. "I got a copy of the tape and damn near wore it out trying to learn all those licks. So that was my first real exposure to chromatic playing."

In 1971 Bill Emerson left Cliff Waldron's band to join the *Country Gentlemen*, and Ben replaced him. Later that year, Ben left Cliff, and in November 1971 he helped to form the *Seldom Scene* along with John Starling, Tom Gray, Mike Auldridge and John Duffey. With them, Ben has refined his playing, combining the best elements of melodic and Scruggs style.

*The Seldom Scene* with Linda Ronstadt and Emmy Lou Harris

In many ways, the key to Ben's playing can be found in his right hand. Attack-wise, he approaches melodic playing almost like Scruggs style, throwing a lot of bounce and punch into his runs. The bounce probably comes from one of *Jim and Jesse's* fine banjoists, Allen Shelton. The punch undoubtedly stems from Scruggs and Bill Emerson, who had a big influence on Ben in the late 1960s.

Another quality of his right hand work is his use of dynamics, which strongly emphasizes the more important notes and brings the others down almost to a whisper. Dynamics aren't usually applied to melodic runs, but by using them in that context, Ben adds a lot of sensitivity to his playing.

Although a master of the melodic style, (listen to his break on "Cross Country"), he still considers Scruggs to be his "main man"—"The reason I'm not a gung ho melodicist is because I think I'm just basically lazy. It's an awful lot of work for me to sit down and learn those strange licks." In addition, the people he played with when he was learning the style didn't approve of the modern sound, an attitude which could easily have dampened his enthusiasm. Nevertheless, the runs creep into his playing. He likes to intermingle these melodic runs with his Scruggs picking, as his breaks to "Muddy Water" and "Gardens and Memories" demonstrate.

Here's an all-purpose run from "Gardens and Memories" which Ben plays against an F chord. It also works nicely for a G or C chord:

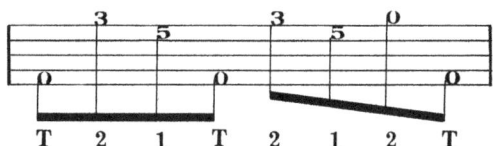

This next lick is one of Ben's trademarks. It's basically chromatic and very easy to play:

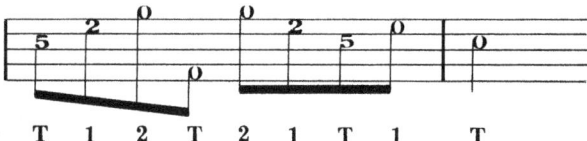

Since Ben uses it in so many different contexts, see if you can figure out your own applications for it.

Obviously, Ben isn't confined to one style of playing: "I don't really feel like you have to stick to one style. I think you hear things in everybody's playing that you like. If I hear something I like—I don't care who's doing it—I'll sit down and try to learn it. And if you can't learn it the way they did it, I'll learn it the way I can do it that's similar. I try to play what feels comfortable."

## Muddy Water

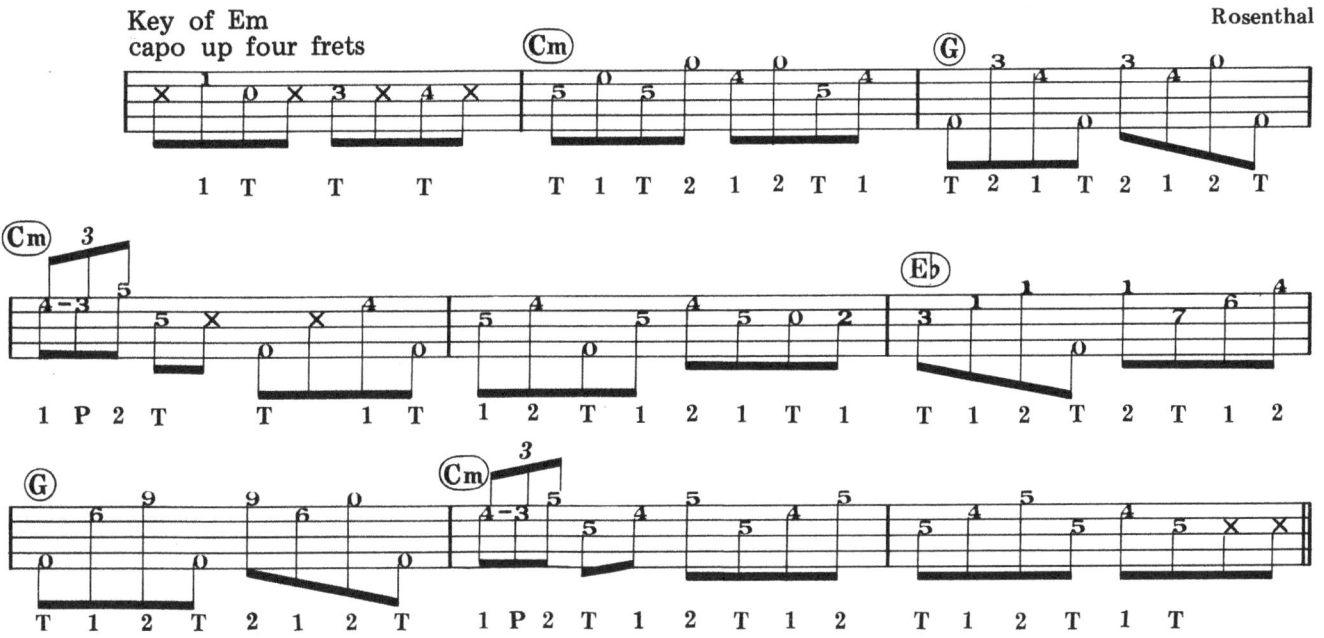

© Lizzie Lou Publications, Inc. All Rights Reserved. Used by Permission.

From the Seldom Scene *Act 3*, Rebel Records SLP-1528

## Gardens And Memories

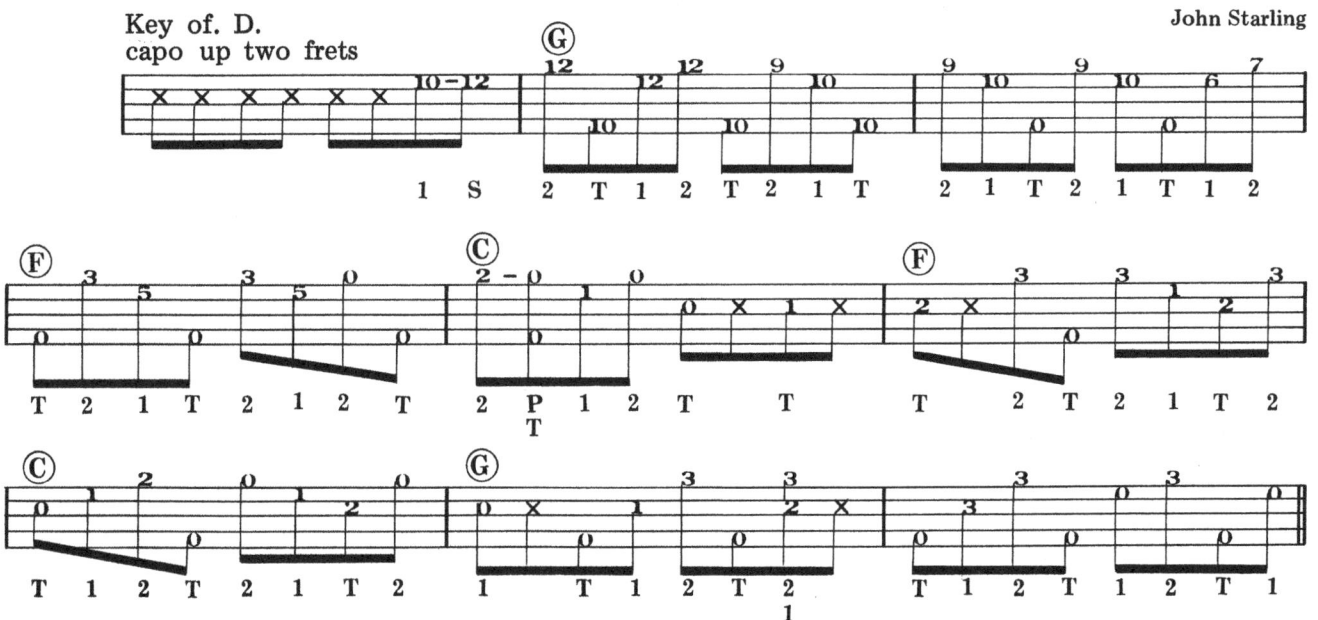

Property of Zap Publishing Company. All Rights Reserved. Used by Permission.

From the Seldom Scene *Act 2*, Rebel Records SLP-1520

# Cross Country

Ben Eldridge and Cliff Waldron

Key of A
capo up two frets
Part A

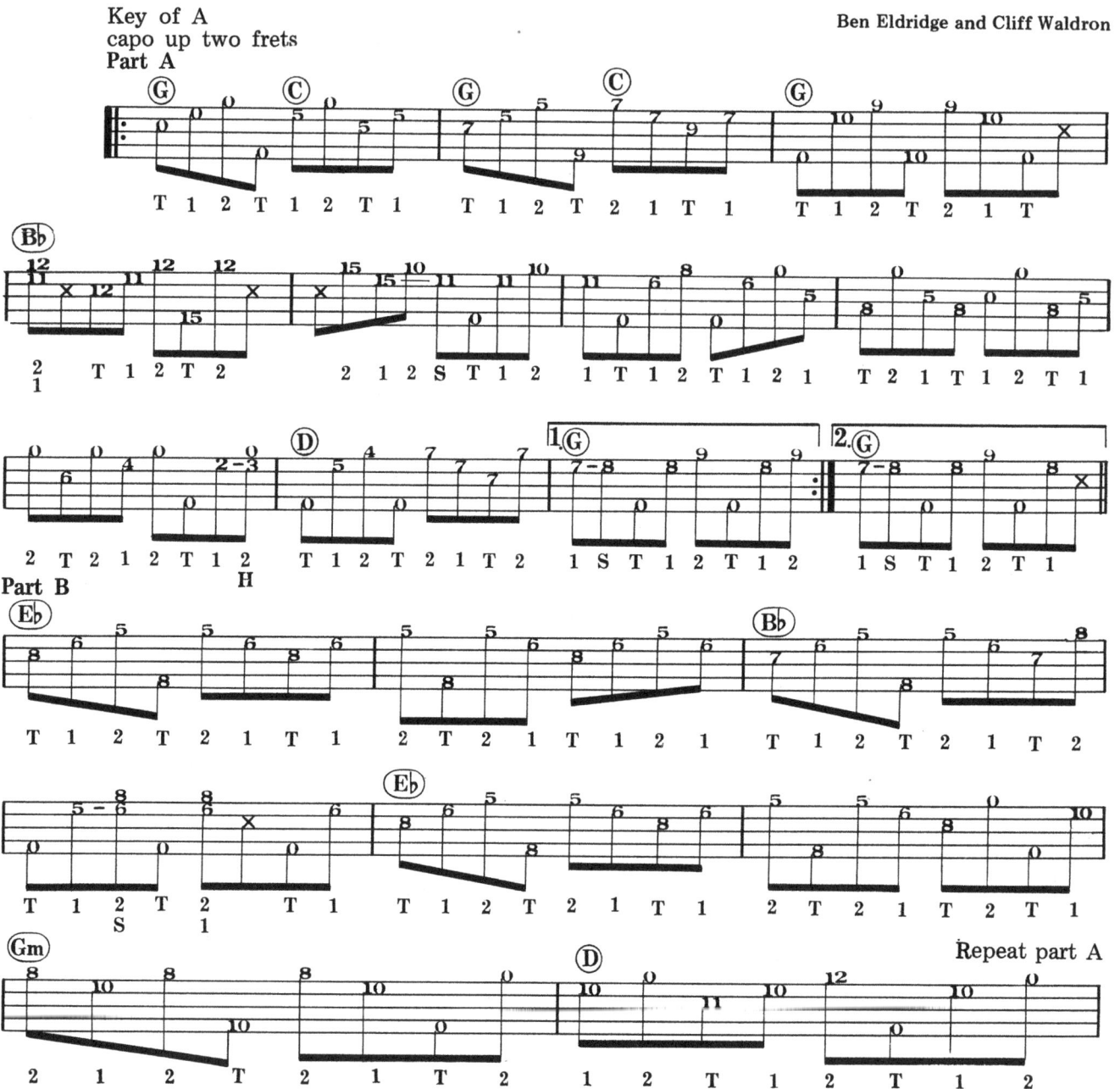

© Zap Publishing Company. All Rights Reserved. Used by Permission.

From Cliff Waldron *Right On*, Rebel Records SLP-1496

JACK HICKS

Over the years Bill Monroe has had a number of fine banjoists pass through his band, including Earl Scruggs, Don Reno, and Bill Keith. In 1972 a young player named Jack Hicks came to work for Bill, making a strong impression with his melodic-chromatic playing and his thorough understanding of the more traditional bluegrass style.

Born in Louisa, Kentucky, in 1952, Jack's family soon moved to Ashland, Kentucky. There he attended high school, and with the inspiration of his band director became deeply involved in music, playing drums, tuba, and string bass in the high school band. Around this time Jack's father, a banjo picker, taught him the rudiments of Scruggs style via "Cripple Creek," and from that point on he was hooked.

For the next few years Jack absorbed the styles of Earl Scruggs, Allen Shelton, Sonny Osborne and Eddie Adcock, but as his playing progressed, he realized that he needed to find new techniques: "I played square dances a long time and the fiddle player would play a fiddle tune; but if you took a banjo break you weren't playing the actual notes. So I thought I might as well get into that, and I started working out those notes." Carl Jackson pointed him in the right direction by showing him his first melodic licks. In addition he listened closely to Bill Keith and Bobby Thompson in order to get a better understanding of the fiddle tune style. Armed with this knowledge, he began to develop his own version of the melodic approach, putting it to good use with Del Reeves, *Jim and Jesse*, and Bill Monroe.

One of the important things he learned from Monroe was how to play the right thing at the right time.... "He more or less taught me how to place licks." Jack's breaks on "Love Come Home," from Bill Monroe's *Father and Son* album (MCA 310) and "Dixieland for Me" from *Buck White and the Downhomers* (County 735) have him inserting blues and chromatic runs tastefully into a Scruggs setting. Here's one of Jack's better known runs which appears in both songs as well as several others. To show its versatility he sometimes uses it against a I chord and other times against a IV chord. Notice also the syncopation at the end of the first measure:

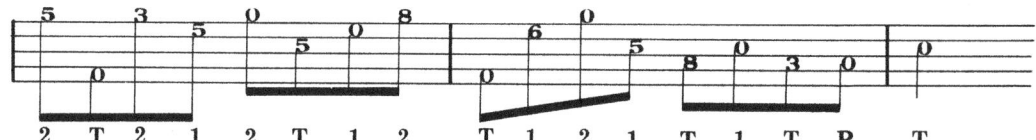

Another one of Jack's trademarks is his use of fancy tags to finish his solos. This next one contains three triplets in a row to produce a spectacular barrage of notes.

Besides being an exciting player on his improvised breaks, he is also a fluid and interesting fiddle tune player. His break to "Indian Blood" is chock full of suprising touches. The first thing you'll notice when you listen to it is that he's using muted banjo, which complements the almost somber feeling of the tune. This feeling is also characteristic of some of Bill Monroe's music, and his influence is strongly evident in this break. You can hear Monroe's touch in the general nature of the melody, and also in the rhythmic kicks at the beginning of the A and B parts. Jack uses harmonics to echo these kicks in the fifth bar of Part B. These harmonics and the use of muted banjo set up a nice textural contrast, not only within the tune, but also within the overall context of the record.

One other interesting point is the positioning of the chord changes in the last three bars of the B part. Instead of falling at the beginning of the measure, they occur in the middle. This positioning creates a feeling of tension because your ear is ready to hear one thing and something else happens instead. Besides all this, the song is really a joy to play. The Gm tuning makes the notes easy to reach and keeps the melody flowing smoothly.

Jack's version of "Gray Eagle," learned during his stint with Monroe, also shows off his considerable fiddle tune technique, but not at the expense of his feeling for the music. . . . "I just pick whatever I feel. I don't play the same thing twice very often. It'll change up a little bit each time. One day I might feel different than the way I do the day before. I guess if I couldn't feel it, I wouldn't pick it."

# Indian Blood

Key of Am
tuning: GDGB♭D
capo up two frets
Part A

Buck White

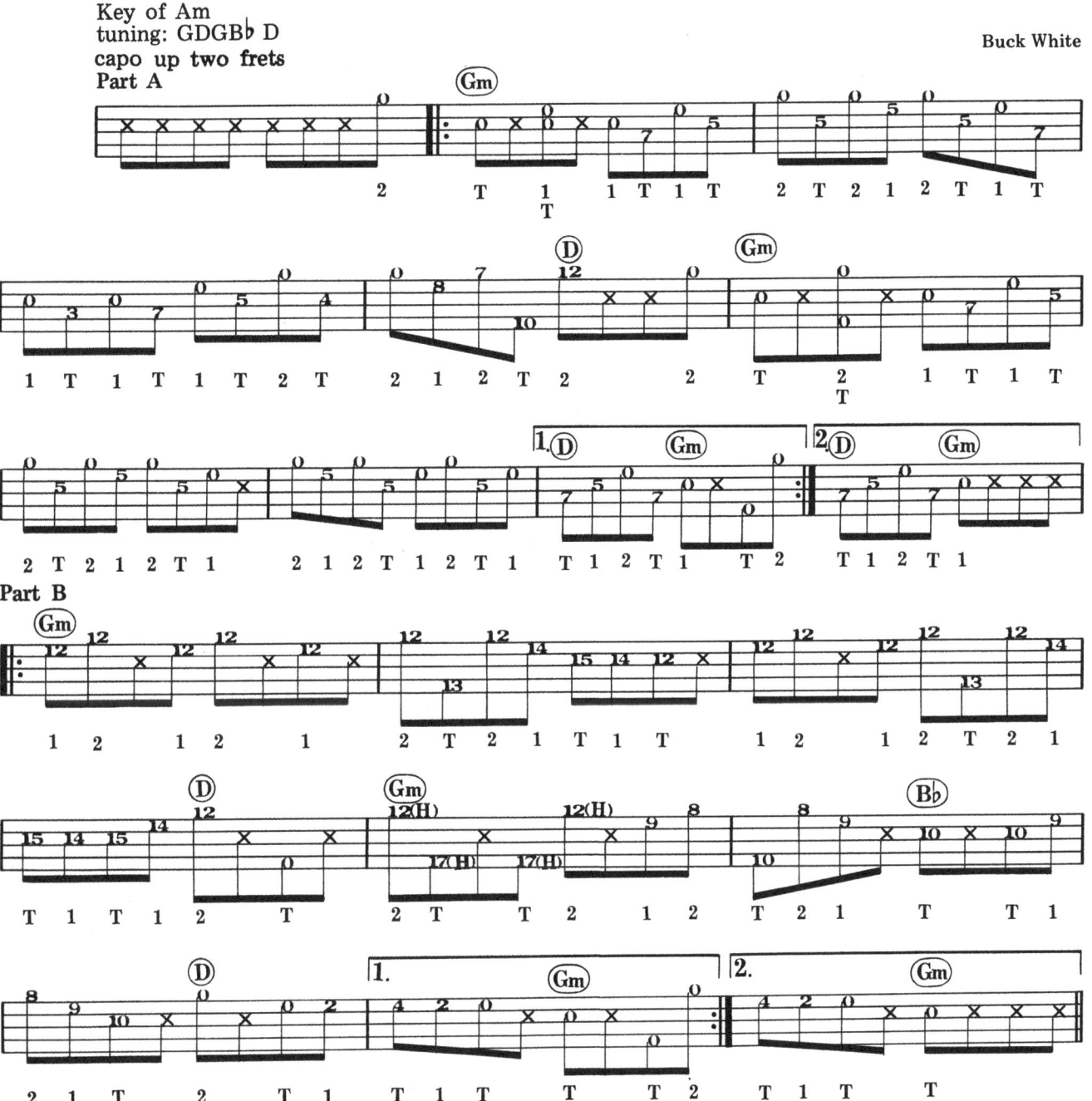

© Buckshot Music Publishing Company. All Rights Reserved. Used by Permission.

From *Buck White and the Downhomers*, County 735

# Gray Eagle

Traditional
Arranged and adapted by Jack Hicks

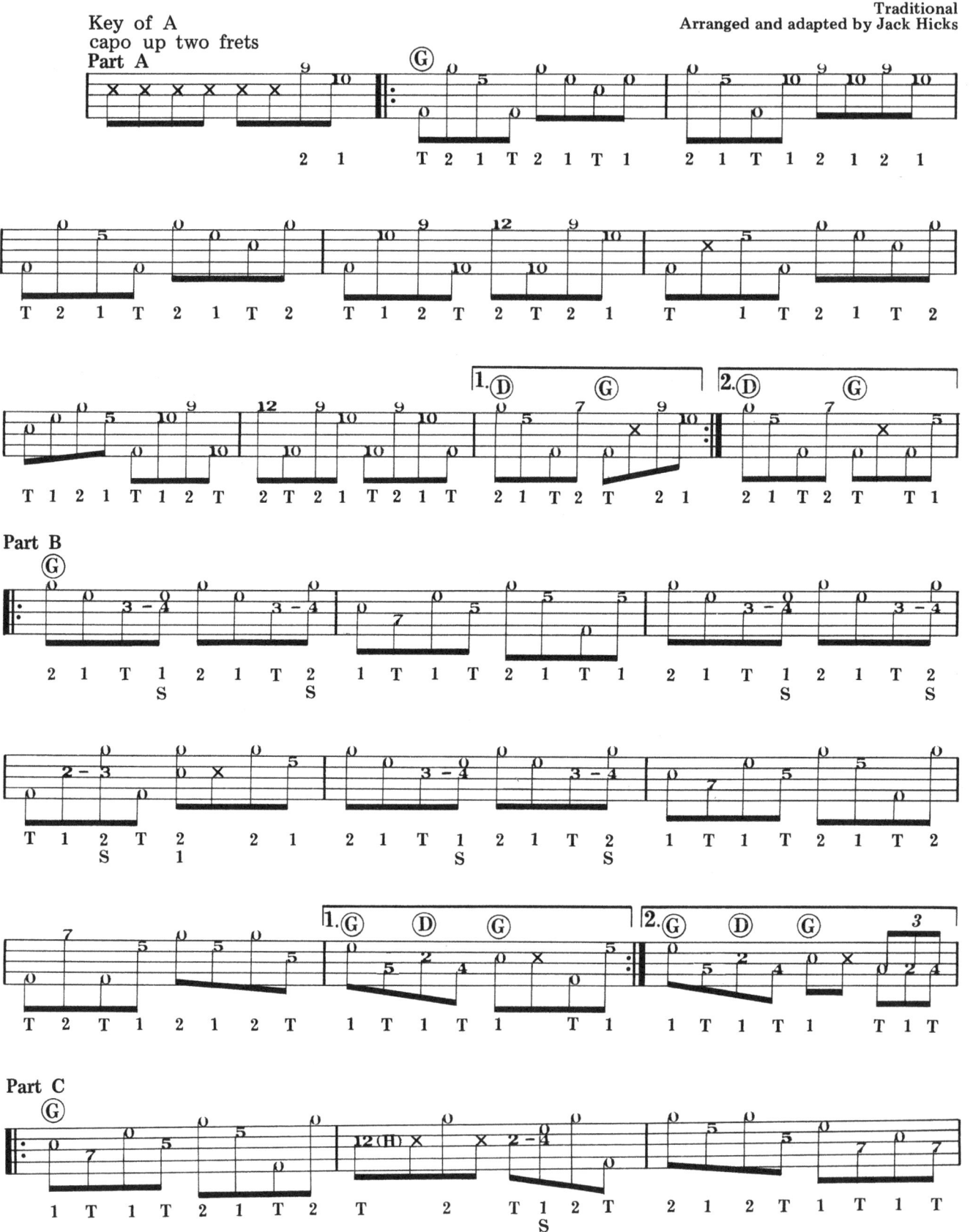

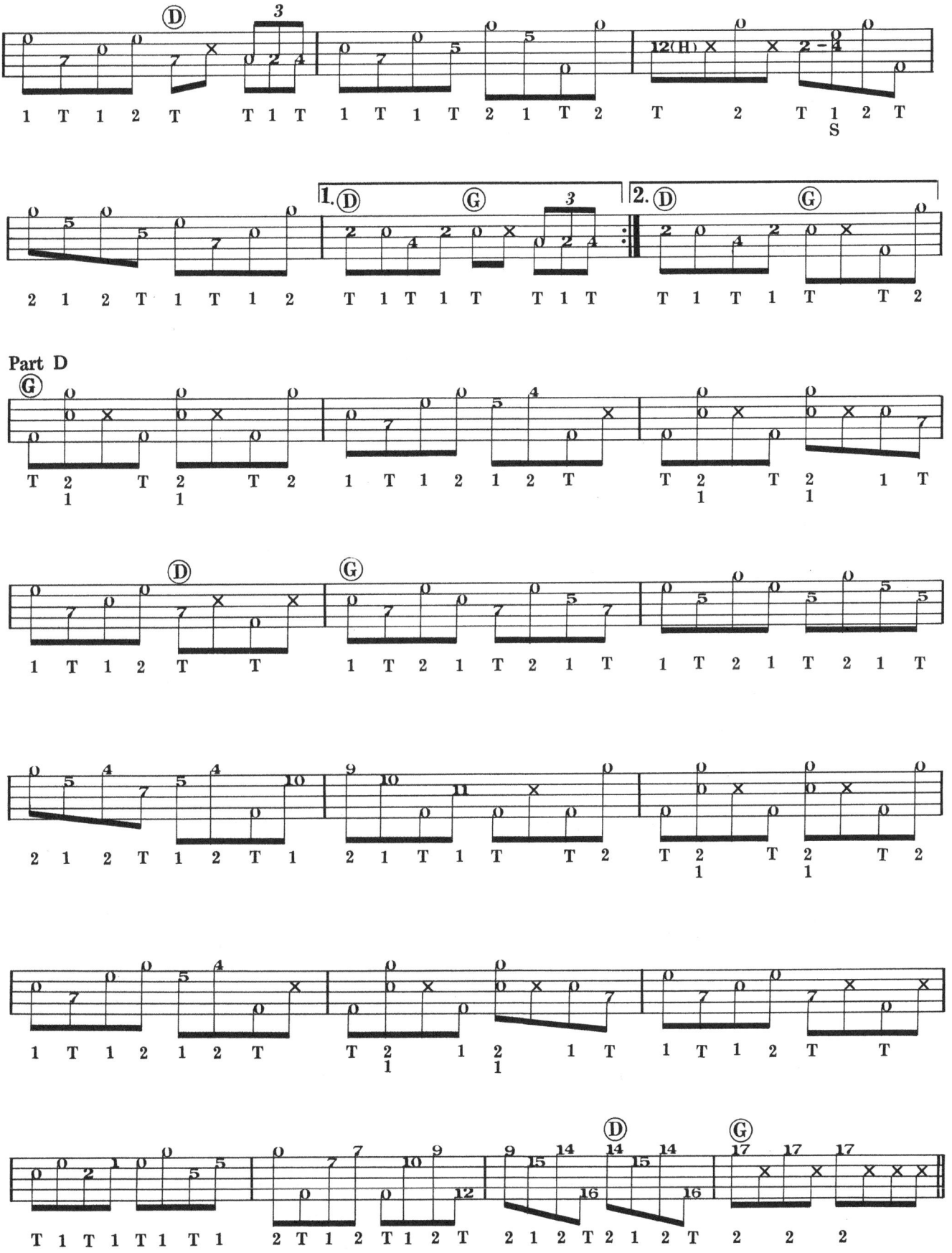

# CARL JACKSON

In live appearances with *Jim and Jesse*, Glen Campbell, and on his own records, Carl Jackson has shown himself to be one of the most solid and devoted melodic players in bluegrass. He has an impeccable sense of time and knows how to be inventive within the fairly rigid form of the fiddle tune.

Carl started playing banjo when he was nine years old and took four or five lessons from a man named Bud Rose. "I was living in Mississippi, but he lived in Alabama. I traveled about sixty miles two or three times a week." One of the most important things that Bud taught him was the need to stress clarity and rhythm in his playing. "When I first started picking, he taught me to play it clear. Never play anything fast until you can play it slow. If I've written something, I'll play it slow until I get to where I can do it and add the speed to it." After a short while Bud left and Carl was forced to learn from records.

He listened mostly to Earl Scruggs and Allen Shelton until he discovered Bill Keith and Bobby Thompson. "I started learning chromatic stuff when I was with *Jim and Jesse* (at the age of 17) which was in 1969, and I think the first tune I learned was Keith's version of "Devil's Dream." Stylistically that was a turning point for Carl. From then on he became primarily a melodic player. "There are certain times when you have the feeling and you just want to play Scruggs stuff. But I really have to prefer playing the straight melody. I love that."

Although Carl likes to stick to the melody, he's also adept at throwing his own licks into fiddle tunes. The licks may not actually be part of the melody, but they always seem to fit.

This blues lick, found in the last few bars of "Bill Cheatham," points this out.

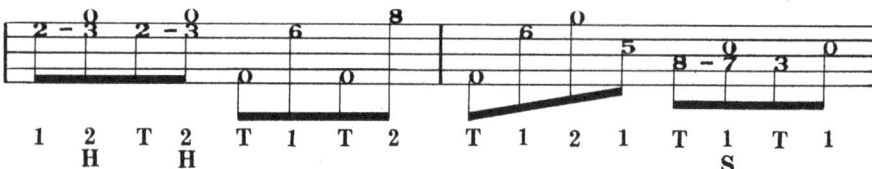

The blues notes contrast nicely with the rest of the tune which has a basically major feel.

Another lick you can extract from "Bill Cheatham" is based on this Keith-oriented lick:

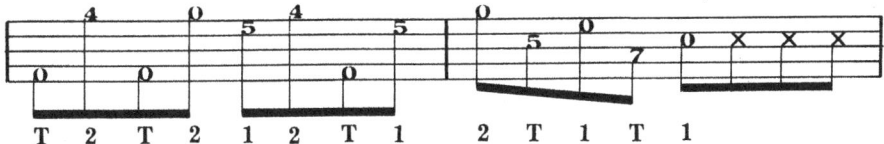

Carl's version is almost identical. However, by changing his left hand position for the first four notes he uses a series of forward rolls to give the run more drive:

Like "Bill Cheatham," "Done Gone" is a traditional fiddle tune, and Carl's playing on it is fairly straightforward. What is interesting, though, is his use of the Gm tuning which makes it easy to play in both B♭ (the A part) and Gm (the B part). These two keys are compatible because Gm is the *relative minor* of B♭. That is, Gm has the same notes in its scale as B♭ has in its scale. The only difference is that the B♭ scale starts on the B♭ note:

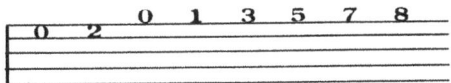

and the Gm on the G:

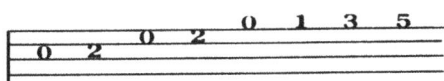

(These are written out for Gm tuning.)

An easy way to determine the relative minor of any major key is by finding the sixth degree of the scale in that key. In the key of G, for instance, the relative minor is Em, and in C it's Am. (You can check the chord chart in the chapter on Basic Chord Positions for help in finding the relative minor of other keys.)

Now try these tunes and see why Carl Jackson is the respected melodicist he is:

# Bill Cheatham

Key of A
capo up two frets

Part A

Traditional
Arranged by Tony Trischka in the style of Carl Jackson

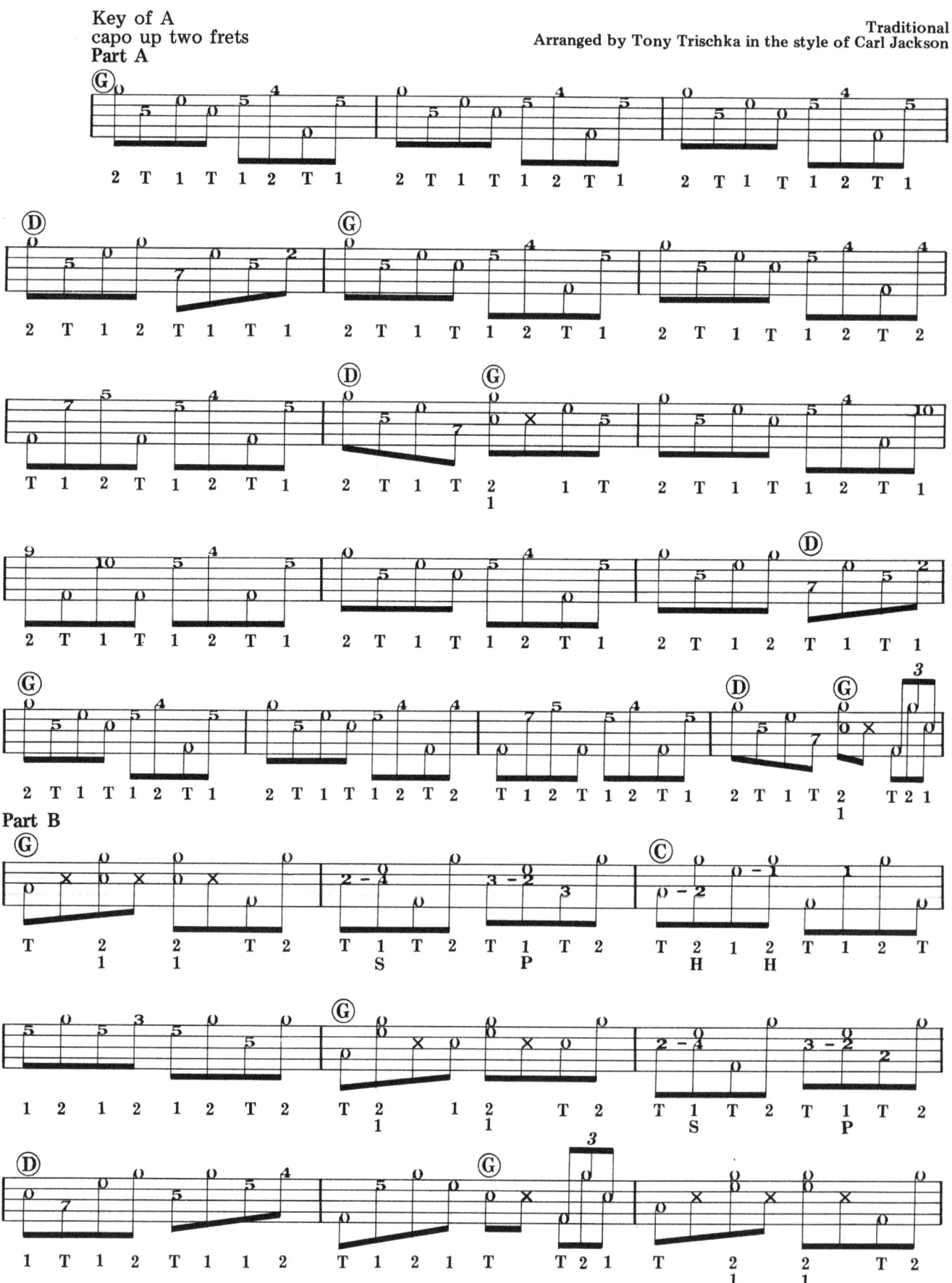

A similar version of this tune can be found on Carl Jackson *Bluegrass Festival*, Prize Records PRS 498-02

# Done Gone

Traditional
Arranged by Tony Trischka in the style of Carl Jackson

Key of B♭
tuning: B♭ DGB♭ D

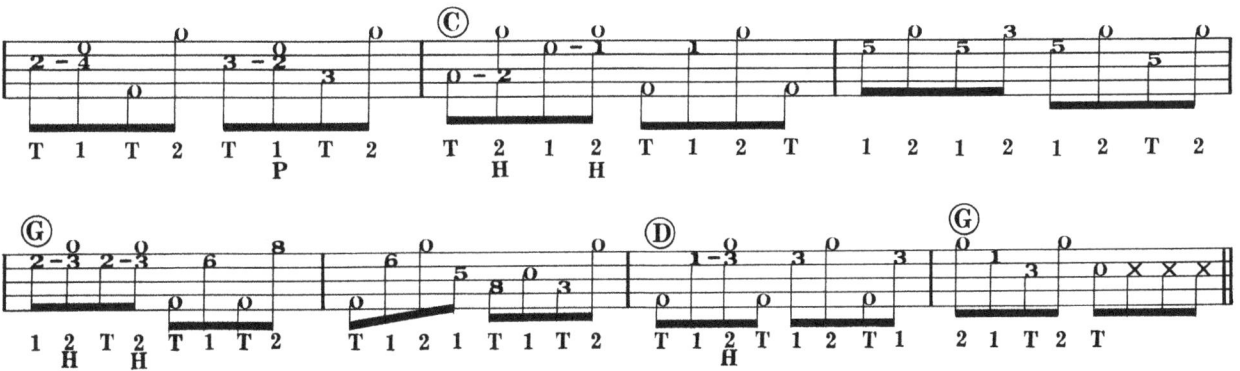

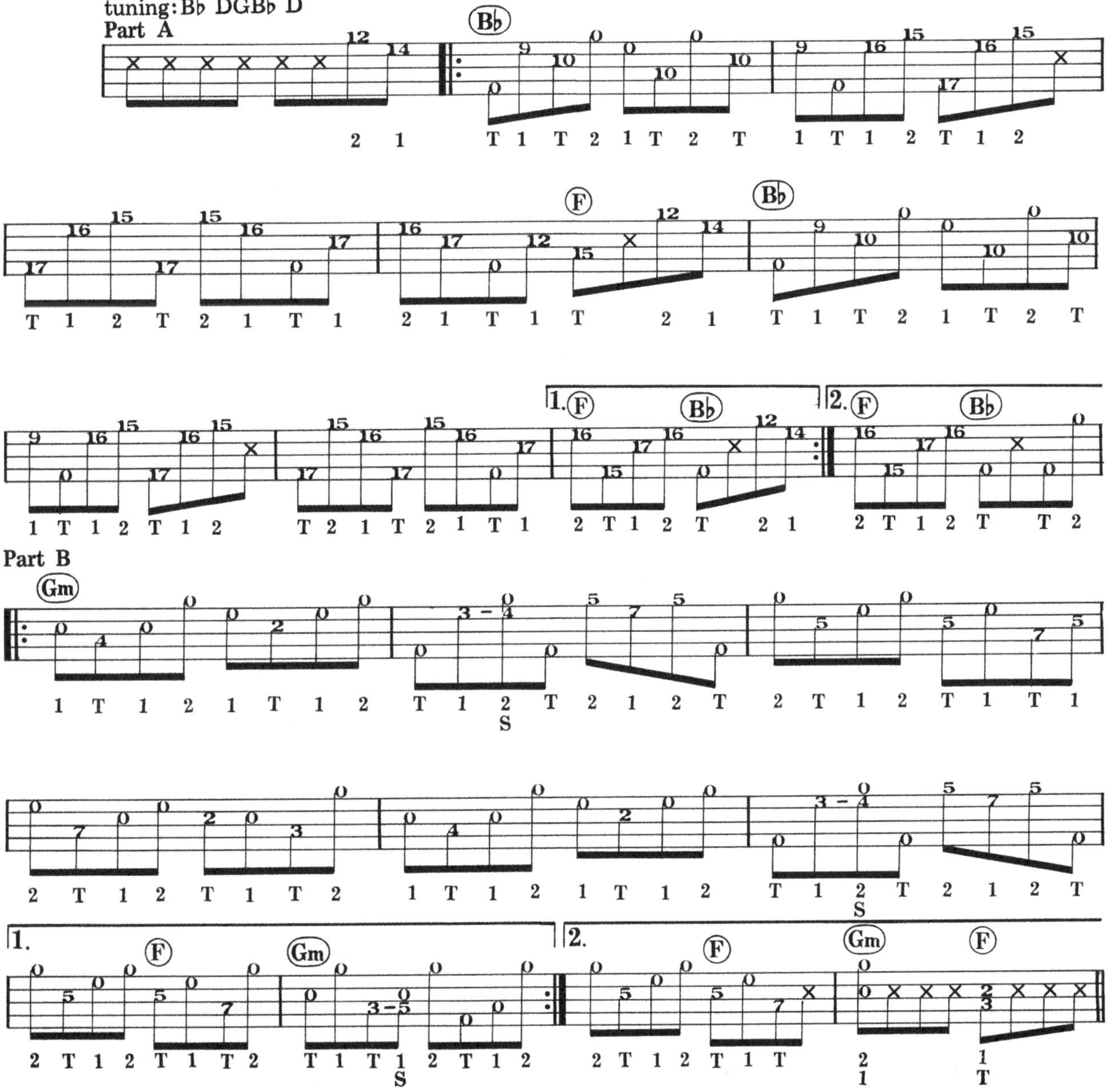

A similar version of this tune can be found on Carl Jackson *Bluegrass Festival*, Prize Records PRS 498-02

85

## COURTNEY JOHNSON

*The Newgrass Revival*/L to R: Courtney Johnson, Curtis Burch, Sam Bush and John Cowan

Courtney Johnson is probably best known for his ascending and descending blues lines, plus his adaptation of fiddle licks to the banjo. These he combines with a love for Scruggs style to produce a richly fused sound.

Courtney was born and raised near Glasgow, Kentucky, and began playing the banjo in 1964. At that time his biggest influence was Ralph Stanley. "I never saw him, but when I started playing that's all the records I had so that's what I listened to. Now, though, it doesn't really sound like I ever listened to him."

In 1969, Courtney began playing with Sam Bush, a dazzling young fiddler from Warren County, Kentucky, and guitarist Wayne Stewart. (Sam and Wayne, along with Alan Munde comprised *Poor Richard's Almanac*.) "Up until then I didn't learn very much. Basically, who I've learned the most stuff from has been Sam, not so much from learning fiddle tunes straight out, but just by picking with him so much."

Courtney also listened a lot to Bill Keith and Alan Munde: "Alan was the first good banjo player I was ever around. When I was around him mostly I was picking stuff sort of like him but then I branched off and started doing what I could do best. No sense trying to copy somebody else."

In the early 70s Courtney got together with Sam Bush, Ebo Walker and Curtis Burch to form the *Newgrass Revival*, one of the first groups to combine rock-oriented material with a bluegrass feel. The two songs included here were recorded by them and indicate how much Courtney favors the melodic approach: "Lots of times when I'm playing, it comes more natural to me than Scruggs style. I like things with more notes, such as jazz. I really dig that. I've listened to John McLaughlin a lot. I just like things with really weird melody lines." You can hear this plainly in his break to "Cold Sailor," which contains this startling lick borrowed from Vassar Clements:

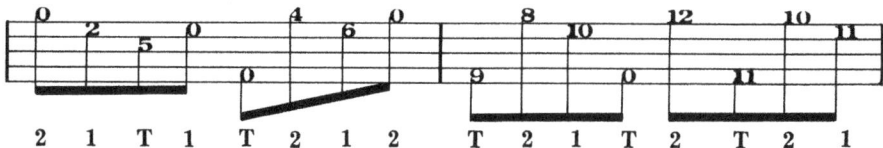

You can use this run in almost any context to lead from a G to a C chord.

Bill Keith's influence can be heard in the eighth bar, where his famous A lick from "New Camptown Races" pops up.

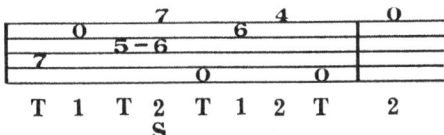

The rest of "Cold Sailor" is fairly Scruggs-oriented except for the long descending blues run at the end. This run, and others like it, make up an important part of Courtney's sound. Sam Bush is responsible for getting him more interested in these blues forms, but only in a general way. . . . "It's not meant to be taken from anyone else. I like blues a lot and I guess it just comes out."

His playing on "Lonesome Fiddle Blues" reflects this interest. The break is totally melodic and sticks pretty close to the original version as played by Vassar Clements. Courtney gives most fiddle tunes a literal treatment, which is probably a result of his spending so much time with Sam.

Even with this heavy involvement in melodic playing, he's careful not to overdo it. In speaking of Scruggs, Courtney comments, "He has so much taste, and he knows what to leave out and what not to. If you're a Scruggs player you have to be able to do that. Melodic picking is the same way. You've got to feel what you're doing for it to come out right."

Courtney Johnson

# Cold Sailor

Key of D
capo up seven frets

Jim Smoak and Steve Brines

© 1971 Experience Publishing (Worldwide). All Rights Reserved. Used by Permission.

As played on *The Newgrass Revival*, Starday Records SLP 482-498

# Lonesome Fiddle Blues

Key of Em
tuning: ADGBD
capo up two frets
Part A

Millie Clements

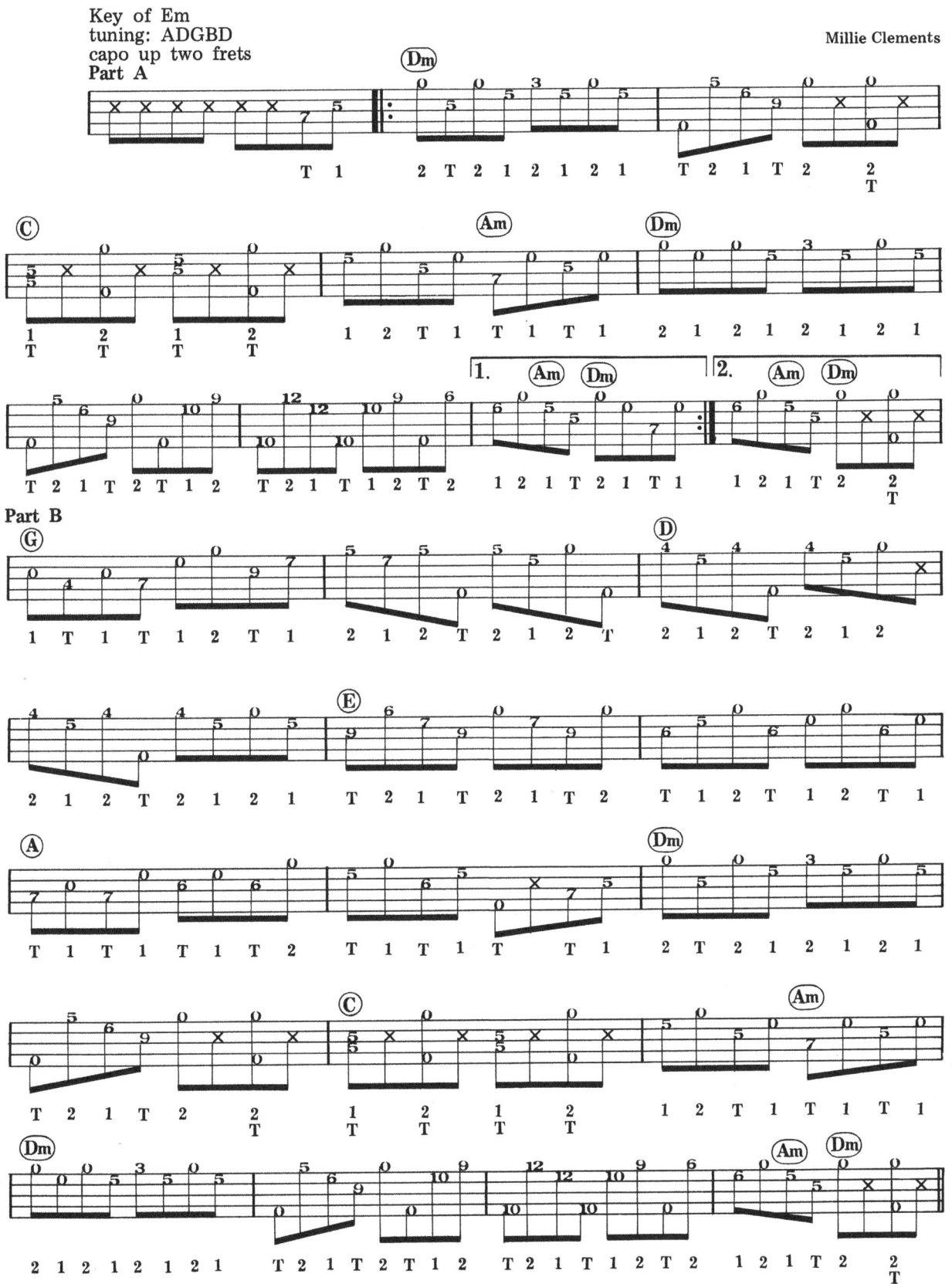

© Vassar's Music. All Rights Reserved. Used by Permission.

As played on *The Newgrass Revival*, Starday Records SLP 482-498

# VIC JORDAN

"As far as a beginner is concerned, get the Scruggs style first, learn good right and left hand placement; then after you feel comfortable, move onto chromatics, but not until." That sums up Vic Jordan's attitude towards banjo playing. Start with the basics.

Vic learned his basics by spending years playing with the men who developed bluegrass music: Jimmy Martin, Bill Monroe, Lester Flatt and *Jim and Jesse.* In each case he adjusted his playing to complement their particular sound, and came out of it all with a style that blends the best aspects of bluegrass banjo. "I like a combination. I like good, drivey stuff, and then put the little flourishes where I think they'll count the most."

Vic's first banjo was a Bacon Blue Ribbon, given to him by his grandfather. It collected dust until he was twenty-one, at which time he began listening to Scruggs and Reno. Since he didn't have anyone to show him the basics, he had to work on his own. This led to some problems, such as learning songs with the low string tuned down to C instead of D. But things progressed and he began playing in his first bands after joining the Air Force in 1958.

In 1964 he moved to Nashville and got his first professional job with *Wilma Lee and Stoney Cooper.* From there he went on to work with Jimmy Martin, who taught him good timing and drive in a straight Scruggs setting; Bill Monroe, with whom he was able to loosen up and get more into the melodic style (especially on the fiddle tunes); Lester Flatt, whom he joined immediately after the departure of Scruggs; and *Jim and Jesse*, who gave him the most room for melodic experimentation.

All of these influences combined to give Vic his distinctive sound: "I take a little bit of this and a little bit of that, add a few touches of my own here and there, and they tell me I have a style."

The man who most influenced the melodic aspect of this style was Bobby Thompson. Bobby had gone back to work for *Jim and Jesse* in 1964 and that's when Vic met him. "I made a trip or two with *Jim and Jesse*, and Bobby and I got to be pretty good friends. And so I studied his playing a little more then. I mean the stuff that everybody didn't hear him do, kind of sitting in the motel room picking. I was really floored back then, and I guess as far as the chromatic style I've studied Bobby more than anybody." Look at Vic's bluesy introduction to "Jordan's Hornpipe" and you'll see how true this is:

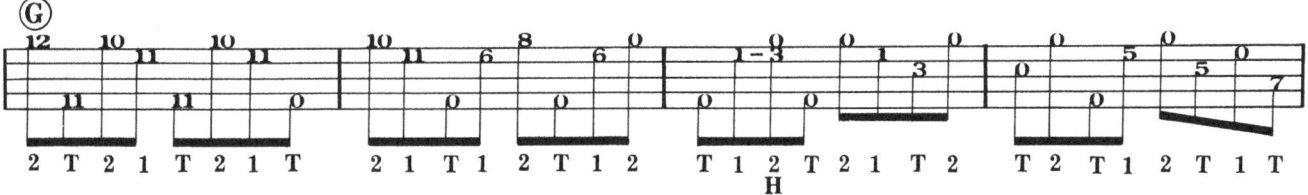

This next run also has the blue Thompson touch and makes for an excitingly propulsive ending, thanks to the triplets. One other thing struck me about the run when I was tabbing it. It's a hybrid. It combines the flashy left hand positions of the melodic blues idiom with the ease of a Scruggsy right hand (it's basically a series of backward and forward rolls). Here Vic has synthesized his traditional and progressive inputs to come up with a hearty new strain.

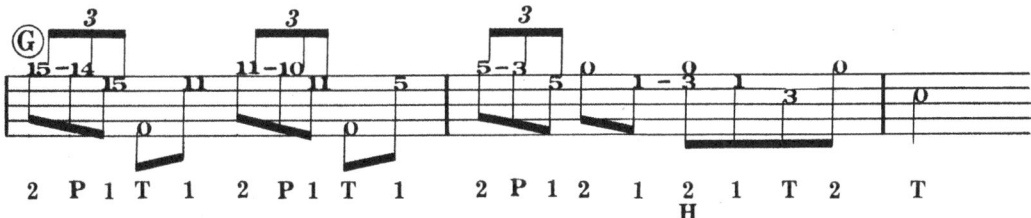

The two runs mentioned above generally stress left hand technique. But here's a lick taken from the B part of "Jordan's Hornpipe" that shows off Vic's inventive use of right hand syncopation.

Vic feels that a well-developed right hand is the key to strong playing. "That's the roll, that's where the time is, that's where the power is, or lack of power (whatever you need). And there are times when you need a lack of power. If there's anything I can't stand, it's an instrument that's going at the same volume constantly no matter what it's doing." This emphasis on the right hand undoubtedly results from his background in the more traditional bluegrass styles which serve as the foundation of the music. In short, "I like Scruggs style as the cake and the melodics are kind of the icing."

# Turkey In The Straw

Traditional
Arranged and adapted by Vic Jordan

Key of G
Part A

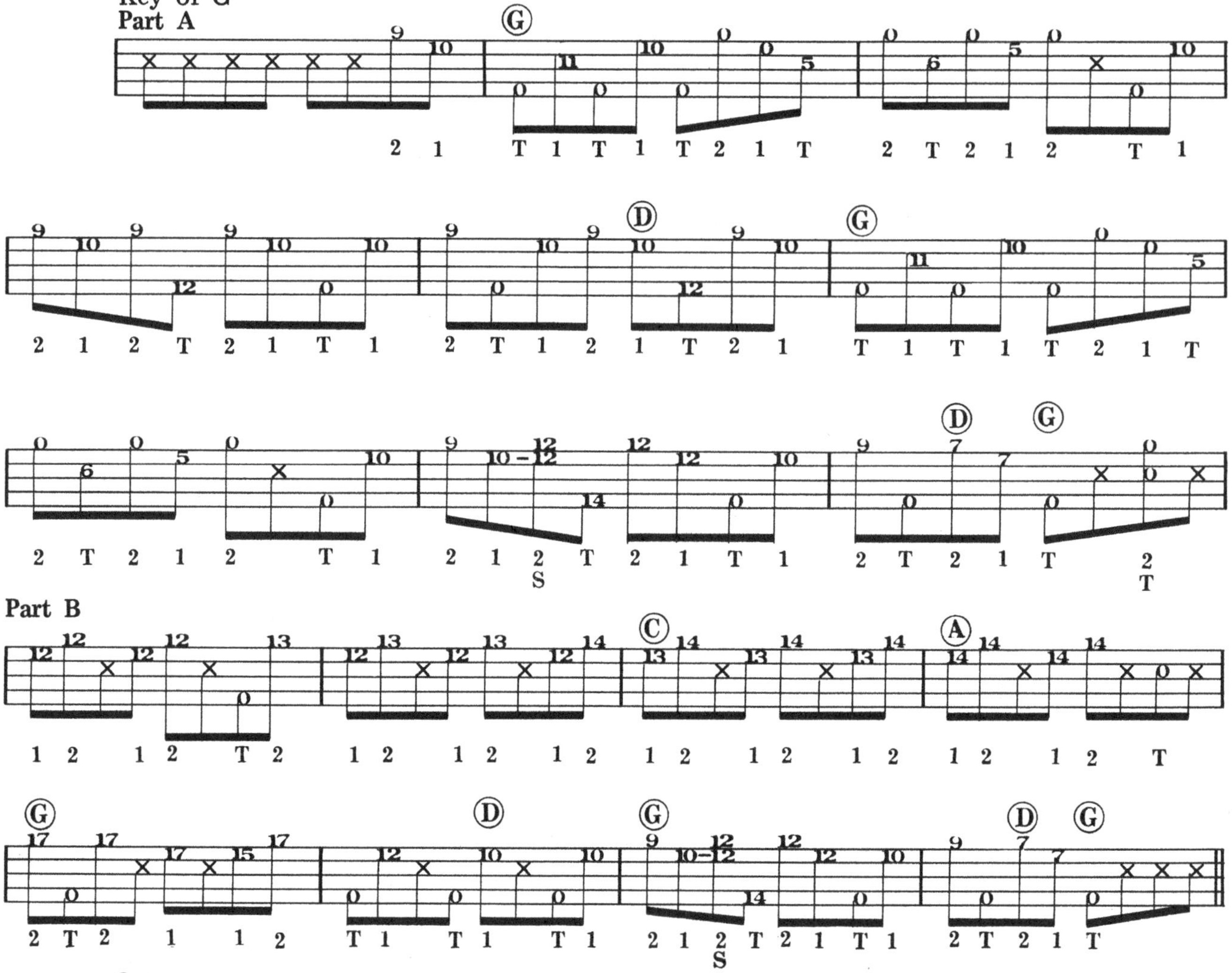

[banjo tablature]

Part B

[banjo tablature]

© Tres-Lynn Publishing Company (ASCAP). All Rights Reserved. Used by Permission.

As played on *Vic Jordan-Pickaway*, API Records API 1027

Vic Jordan with Jesse McReynolds

# Jordan's Hornpipe

Vic Jordan

Key of G
Introduction

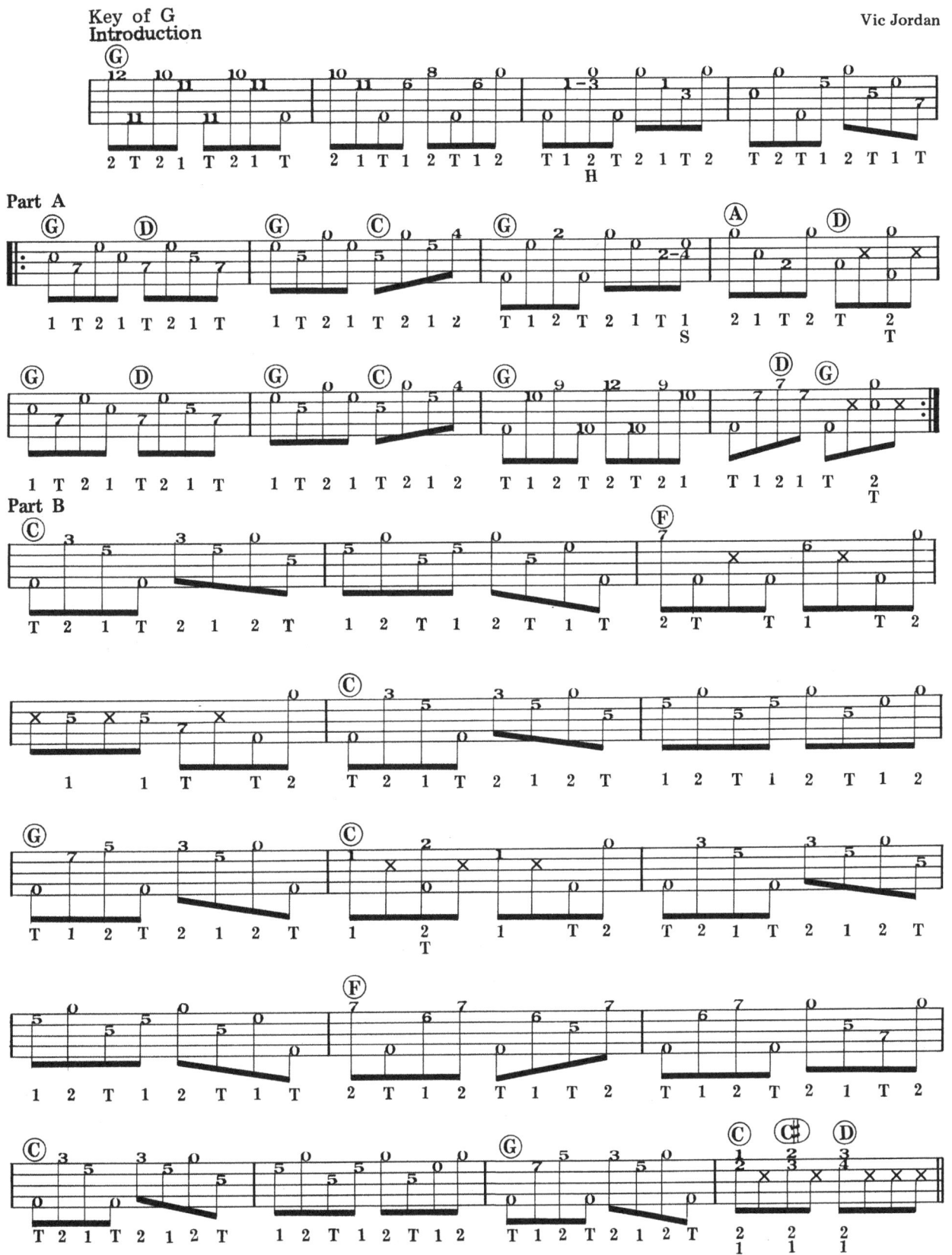

© Tres-Lynn Publishing Company (ASCAP). All Rights Reserved. Used by Permission.

As played on *Vic Jordan-Pickaway*, API Records API 1027

## ALAN MUNDE

Alan Munde is Norman, Oklahoma's gift to bluegrass. When he's on stage he stands stone-faced and silent behind the banjo. But he has a knack for grabbing an audience by sending out an endless stream of notes on a fiddle tune, or by throwing a particularly choice melodic lick into the middle of a driving Scruggs break.

Alan first got interested in music while attending the University of Oklahoma (1964-1969). He played guitar for about a year and then switched to banjo after hearing Pete Seeger and Earl Scruggs. Prize-winning fiddler Byron Berline was also going to the school and he and Alan got together to play in 1965.

Byron did two things for Alan—he introduced him to the playing of Bill Keith via tape, and spurred his interest in Texas-style fiddle tunes. "Byron played them and then I'd try to learn them. But I never had him show them to me note-for-note. Just because I had a fiddler there who played them, I wanted to play them too."

The other strong influence on Alan at this time was Ed Shelton, a fine banjoist from Oklahoma City. "He's the one who taught me how to play music on the banjo. Up until then I just played. When you just learn how to play, you don't really know what to do. He kind of showed me where things go." Ed had a Scruggs-oriented melodic style. "He would work out of a position rather than playing note-for-note. It had a good drive to it but still had the melodic flavor; and I always kind of liked that."

In 1968, Alan met Courtney Johnson at a folk festival in Arkansas. Courtney introduced him to Sam Bush and Wayne Stewart. Alan, Sam and Wayne formed *Poor Richard's Almanac* in Kentucky and put out one excellent record of fiddle tunes for American Heritage. After three months, though, Alan was drafted into the Army.

Upon his return, he went to Nashville to play with Jimmy Martin. "It was pretty rough on me. It was my first time out and I accepted a lot of things he said, and I found a lot of them to be wrong." To play with Jimmy he had to give up his melodic playing, and methodically learn the "Good 'n Country" style of J. D. Crowe and Bill Emerson, two of Jimmy's previous banjoists. "I tried to do it as close as I could to them, but I just got tired of trying to do what someone else had done so much better. After I left him I made up my mind for my own well-being that I wasn't going to sit down to learn off a record again." Alan did benefit from Jimmy in one way, though. "He instilled in me a professional attitude about music. I like to play it as well as I can."

L to R: Bill Monroe, Alan Munde and Jimmy Martin

In 1972, Alan got a call from Byron Berline and Roger Bush who were playing with the *Flying Burrito Brothers*. The *Burritos* had actually broken up but they still had jobs lined up in Europe. So Alan went over to play guitar with a makeshift *Burrito* band and earned enough money to move to California to start *Country Gazette* with Roger and Byron.

With *Country Gazette*, Alan's style crystallized, combining the drive that he taught himself while playing for Jimmy Martin with a strong and clear fiddle tune style. His picking on "Lonesome Blues" is a perfect example of this.

Here Alan takes short blues and chromatic runs and intertwines them with a crisp forward-rolling Scruggs style to result in an incredibly tasteful break. One of the most pleasing licks in "Lonesome Blues" is this combination of chromatic and blues notes which appears in the fourth bar from the end.

Alan's break to "Dusty Miller" is totally melodic and shows how well he adapted the Texas fiddle tune style, which he absorbed from Byron and Sam Bush, to the banjo. A characteristic of this style is the flow of notes which seem to go on uninterrupted from beginning to end. Notice also the chords, which are placed differently than they would normally be in a bluegrass version of this tune.

This break is particularly enjoyable because it's very comfortable to play. Every note of the fiddle tune is there, but there are no difficult left hand reaches or tricky right hand rolls. Also, Alan has included a number of licks which can be applied easily to other songs. Here's one;

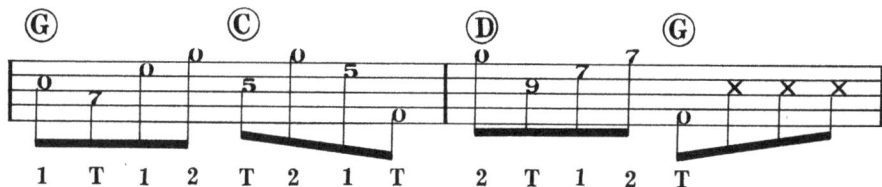

and try this:

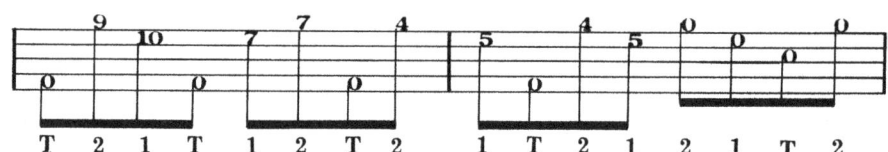

From playing these examples and listening to him on record, you can see that Alan is a fully realized player who never stops creating new and interesting music on the banjo.

# Dusty Miller

Key of A
capo up two frets

Parts A

Traditional
Arranged and adapted by Alan Munde

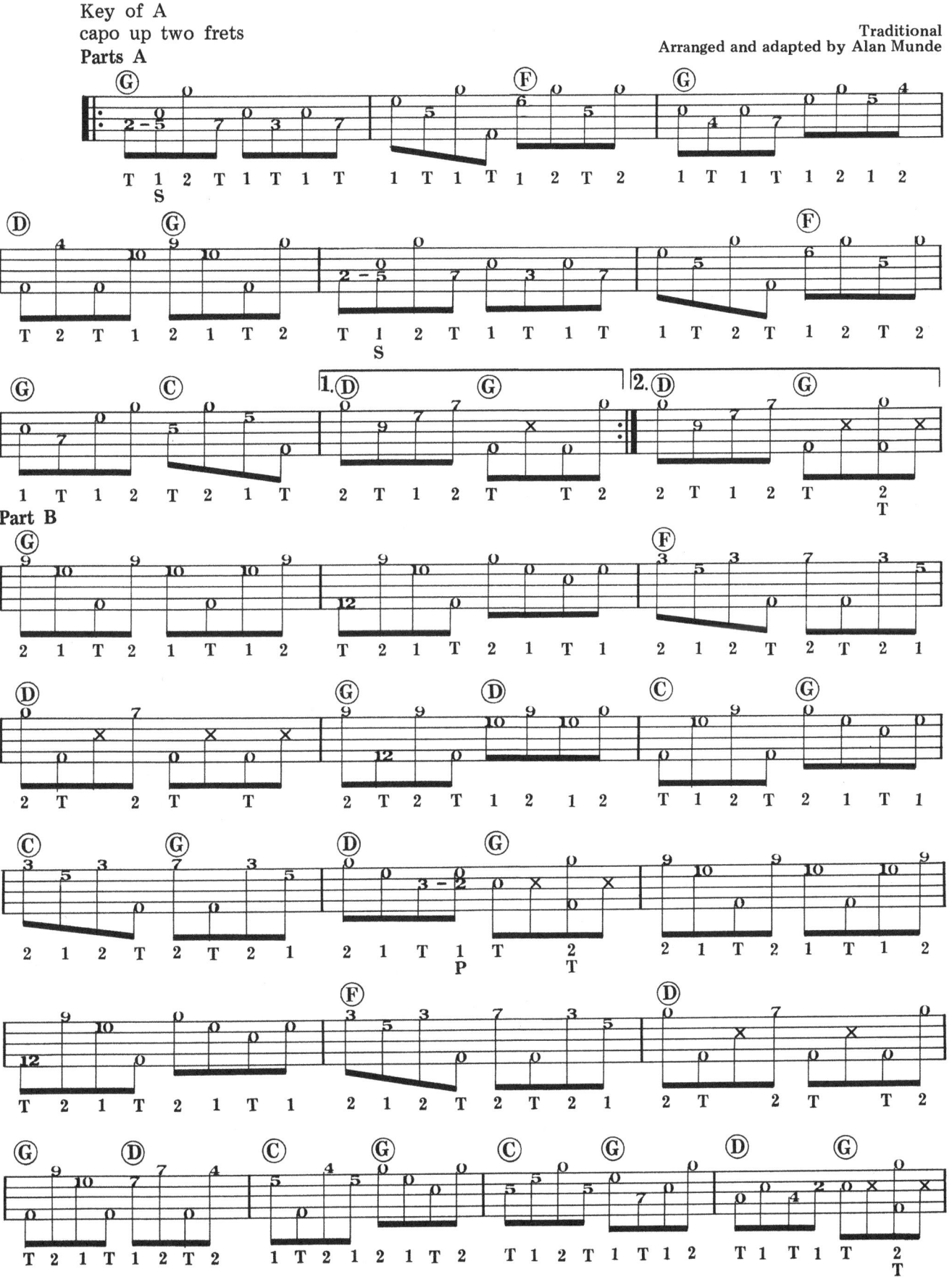

**Part C**

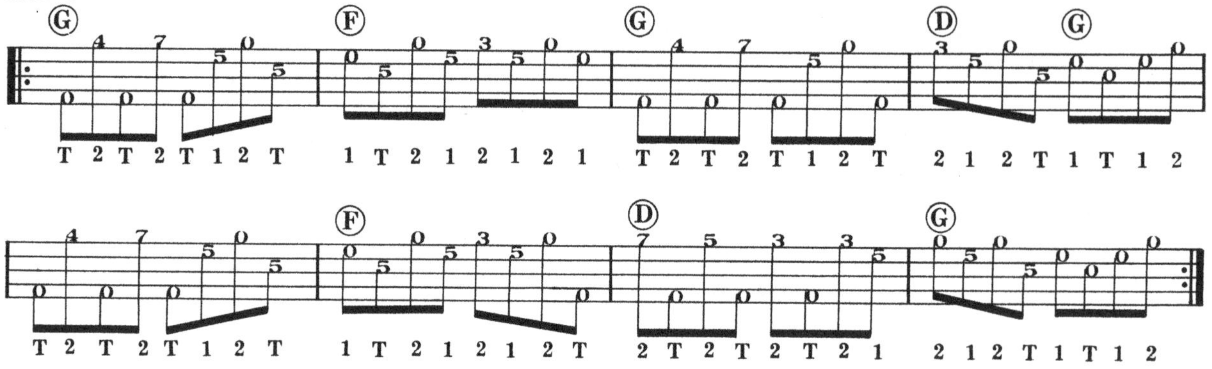

As played on *Poor Richard's Almanac*, American Heritage Records

## Lonesome Blues

H. and N. Pederson

Key of B
capo up four frets

I've got the lone - some blues to - night    Won't you stay and be a friend    that's what I need.    Some - one to hold me tight,    tell me it's al - right.    I've got the lone - some blues to - night.

© Dear Friends Music Company. All Rights Reserved. Used by Permission.

As played on Country Gazette's *Don't Give Up Your Day Job*, United Artists Records UA-LA090-F

# Working Up Songs On Your Own

Up to this point you've had everything pretty much laid out for you. But how do you learn a song off a record or adapt a tune from another instrument to the banjo?

For learning off a record your best bet is to hook a tape recorder up to your stereo system and tape the break you want. (Make sure you're in tune with the song before you start.) You should record at a high speed (7½ i.p.s.) and play back at a slow speed (3¾ or 1⅞ i.p.s.). This will allow you to hear every individual note clearly.

If you're learning from another instrument, such as fiddle, just have the other person play the tune slowly, several notes at a time, until you have it under control.

In either case, the main problem is to figure out what the left hand positions are. With Scruggs style, this isn't too difficult because the positions used for licks are fairly standard. In the melodic style, though, there can be several different ways to get the same notes. Take this G scale for example:

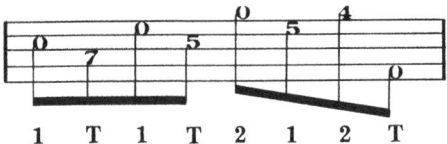

These same notes can also be played this way:

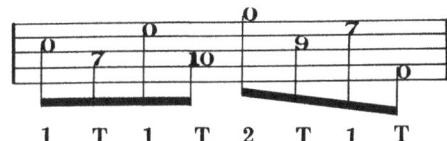

As Bill Keith says, "When you think you know something about the neck, think again. There are probably five positions to play the same thing in, and if you can find them, you're better off."

The idea is to play with economy of movement. In other words, find the easiest way to play the notes you want to play. For instance, if you're learning the beginning of "Sally Goodin," you don't have to jump all over the neck:

You'll have an easier time playing it like this:

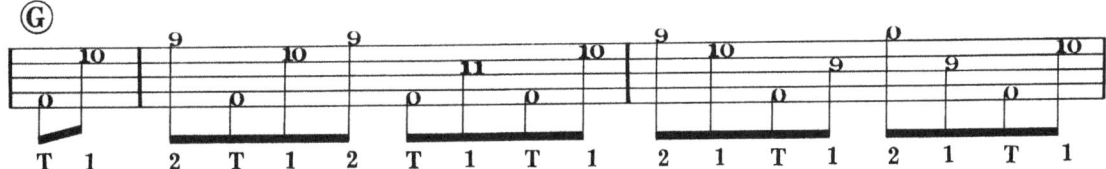

Carl Jackson brings up another point. . . . "What I've always told anybody is play as many open strings as you can and there's always an easier way to do it. Don't let anybody tell you otherwise." Instead of playing this,

A final thing to keep in mind is your tuning. When you're adapting a song from another instrument to the banjo, you may not always want to work out of the normal G D G B D tuning. Another tuning sometimes makes a song easier to play. After all, you shouldn't feel strapped to the G tuning. Experiment a little and you may come up with some interesting results. Courtney Johnson's tuning on "Lonesome Fiddle Blues" and Carl Jackson's on "Done Gone" are good examples of this.

To sum things up, here are some of Alan Munde's thoughts on the subject: "Work it out the easiest way you can. I've seen people who've worked out a tune you've recorded or that they've heard you play, and it's the same notes, but the way they got it is just amazing they ever thought of it. They always say, 'Well, I'll change it.' And I say, 'No, don't do that. If you can play it that way, what's the difference.' So I would say, whatever's comfortable usually works out right."

Butch Robins, one of the most inventive and unheralded melodic players in bluegrass. He has performed with *The Newgrass Revival, Buck White and the Downhomers*, Wilma Lee and Stony Cooper, Bill Monroe, and Harry James.

# Melodic Backup

Melodic playing is usually thought of as a lead style. However, you can also incorporate it into your backup playing. If you're going to do this, be sure to stick to the less flashy runs. Remember, you want to keep things as uncluttered as possible.

The best way to accomplish this is by playing mostly straight-ahead Scruggs licks and throwing in simple melodic runs and fragments more or less for flavor. An effective place to use these runs is during the spaces when the singer stops to breathe, or when a long note is being sustained. Here's a hypothetical down-the-neck backup for "Will the Circle Be Unbroken."

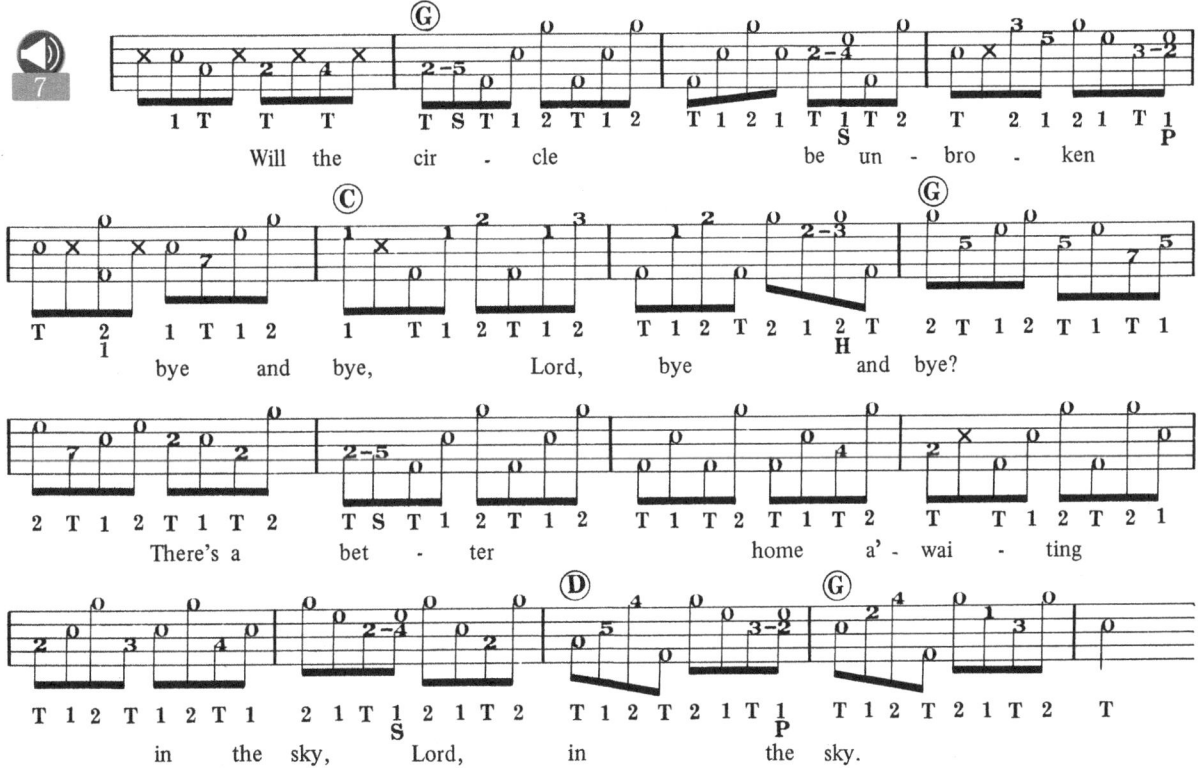

And try this for an up-the-neck backup to "Nine Pound Hammer":

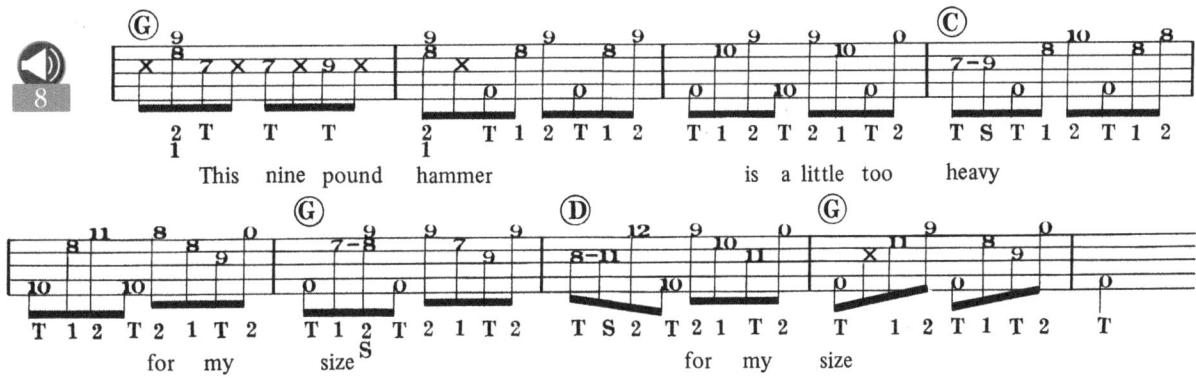

Of course the possibilities for melodic backup are infinite, and these are only two examples. But they should give you some idea of what to aim for. Just listen to the person playing or singing lead and be sensitive to what he or she is doing and you'll have no problem.

# Improvising Melodically

The melodic approach is often looked at as being more of a "composed style" than Scruggs picking. This is especially true with fiddle tunes, which are so worked out that if you make a mistake in the middle, you often have to stop for a few bars until you can get back on the track. Eric Weissberg looks at it this way: "If you get lost, it's like starting a speech all over from the beginning."

But there's no reason why you can't improvise readily in the melodic style. The trick is not to think of a tune in terms of an overall structure, but instead as being broken down into sections. That way if you start to have trouble with a particular section, you can improvise something else to fill the gap. Throughout the book I've isolated various licks which can be used in this way. As you learn more and more tunes, you'll build up a storehouse of these licks and runs in your memory to get you out of tight spots, or to throw in when the urge hits you.

For instance, if you're playing "Red Haired Boy",

and you run into trouble in the third bar, think of a lick in the same key that will smoothly fill up a couple of bars.

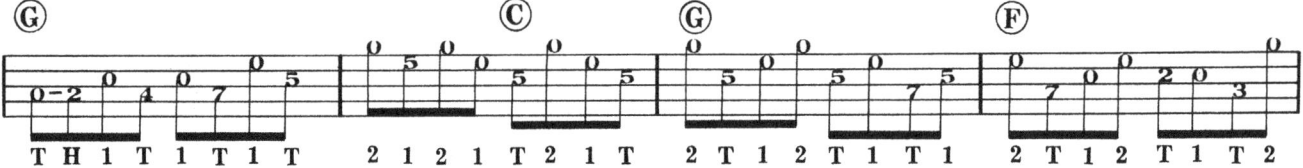

The lick you use should be fairly familiar to you so that you can play it automatically while you concentrate on getting back to the melody of the tune.

Actually, you shouldn't always feel obligated to play the exact melody of a song. Give it something of your own. For example, you can make up your own breaks to fiddle tunes. To do this, you should think of substitute licks that will fit the feel of the song. There are several tricks you can use to get these licks.

If a part of the melody is ascending, make it descend, and vice versa, using the same or similar notes. Bill Keith does this in his break to "Blackberry Blossom." The basic melody is:

He plays it like that the first time through, but the second time he reverses it:

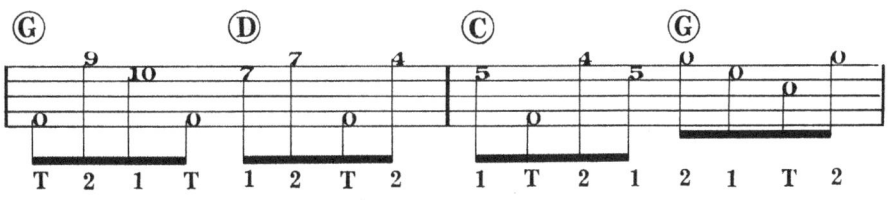

You can also loosen up the melody of a tune by changing selected notes here and there. For instance, take the beginning of "Sally Goodin":

You can change a few individual notes to give it a more chromatic and bluesy feel:

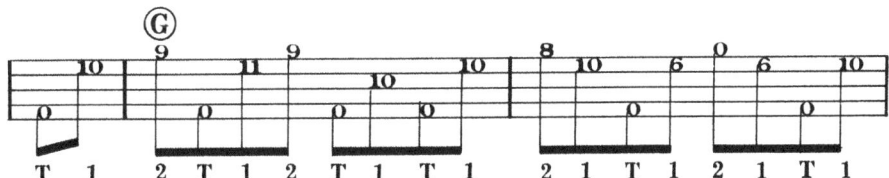

Hopefully, you'll get to the point where you can do this instinctively while you're playing.

Generally, this is easiest to do between the third and eighth frets because you can make ample use of open strings. This will give you the time you need to think of the next fretted note. By moving your finger only one fret, you can completely change the feel of a tune from diatonic to bluesy to chromatic. It all depends on your mood at the time. This variable is what makes improvising so exciting. Sometimes you'll play and nothing of consequence will come out. Other times, though, you'll surprise yourself with music you never knew was inside you. As Courtney Johnson says, "I do things I don't even realize I do. It's a reflex. You hear something in your head and you do it."

Here are some more ways to get to this point. You can improvise entire licks on the spot by simply shifting a familiar lick into a different position. Take this Bobby Thompson-oriented run:

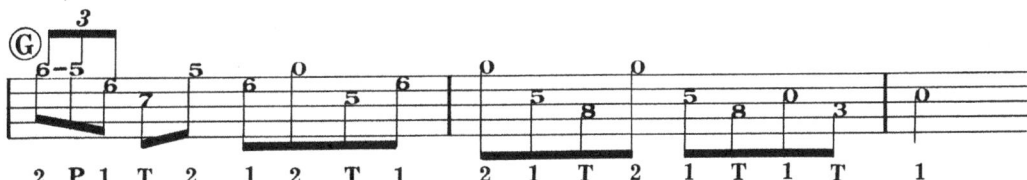

By moving it down two frets, and keeping the same right hand patterns, you can have a workable F run that fits nicely in a tune like "Little Maggie":

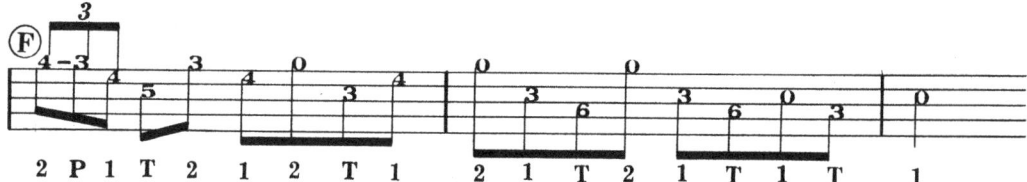

You can do the same sort of thing with this descending G run.

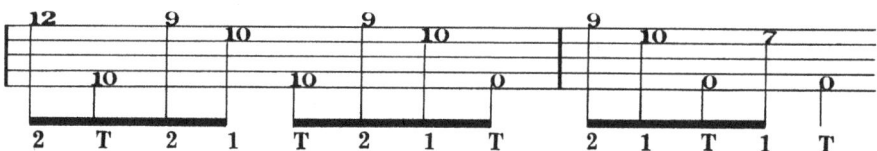

Move it up two frets and you'll get a different, slightly odd sounding G or A run.

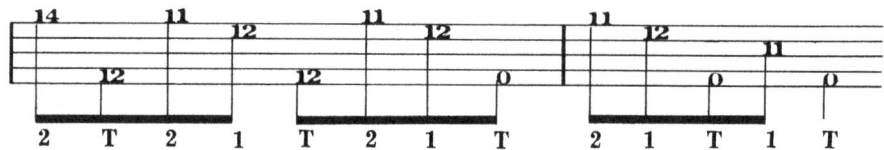

Another way you can improve your improvisatory skills is by learning the scales for the most commonly used keys. Once you're familiar with them you can dissect them and use bits and pieces as the need arises. Here's "Nine Pound Hammer" to demonstrate:

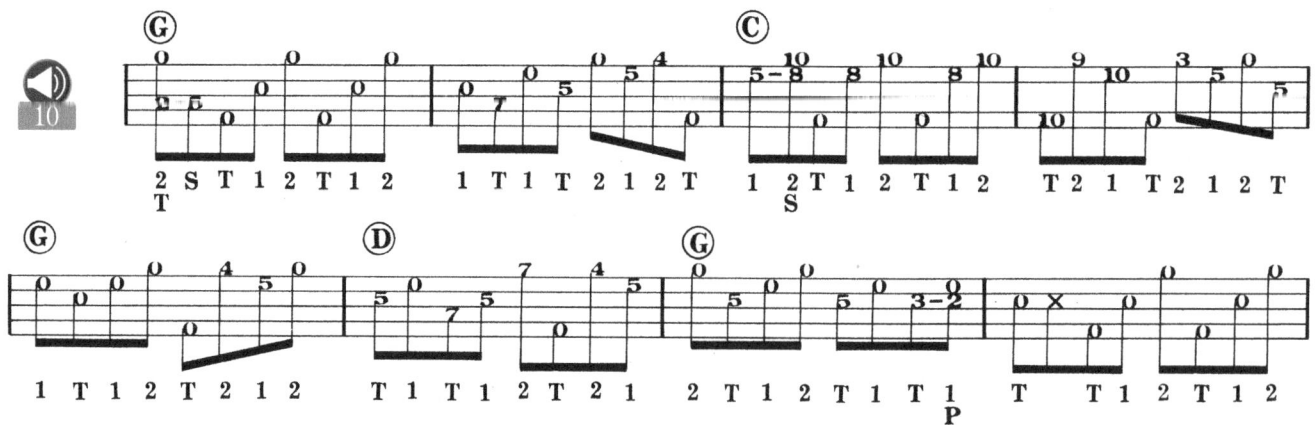

Here I used an ascending G scale for part of the G chord, a descending C scale against the C, and fragments of a G scale for the last D and G chords. Again, you should get to the point where you can do this sort of thing off the top of your head.

You can also improvise with the right hand by fooling around with different rolls. If you want syncopation, try playing a forward or backward roll several times in a row while changing your left hand position. Run through this beginning of "John Hardy" to get some ideas.

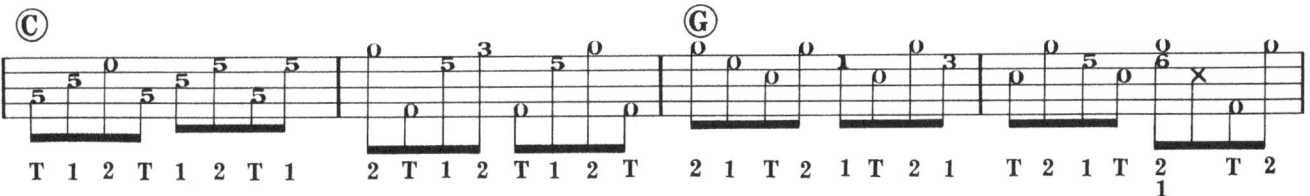

Of course you can use other rolls as well, but I'll let you experiment with that yourself.

One final way you can come up with new licks and runs is by looking beyond the normal bluegrass inputs. Jack Hicks, for instance, has borrowed ideas from Tchaikovsky. Bobby Thompson has also gone to other types of music to get a different slant on things. In fact, I've heard him play a version of "Dueling Banjos" in which he inserts the main theme to the "Grand Canyon Suite." Jazz can also offer a lot of possibilities for adaptation to the banjo. Just keep your ears and mind open and you can really spice up your playing.

In the long run it's all up to you. I've given you a few hints on improvising that will hopefully lead you into new musical territory on the banjo. So don't let yourself get caught up in old patterns. The possibilities are limitless, and as your technique and imagination expand, you can start exploring the depths of your own creative potential.

Pat Cloud with *Country Store* (Jimmy Gaudreau-mandolin, Keith Whitley-guitar). Pat is a legend on the East Coast and a source of amazement on the West (these days he lives in San Francisco). His reputation has been built on his incredibly free melodic style which incorporates a large body of scales, modes, and chords not often heard on the banjo. He combines this technical knowledge with a supercharged attack and applys it not only to conventional bluegrass tunes, but also to bebop and swing music. He does it all convincingly and if you get a chance to hear him, he'll definitely open your ears to some new sounds on the banjo.

# Fiddle Tune Finale

This final section contains some of the most popular fiddle tunes in the melodic repertoire. The only exceptions are the last two songs, which are currently dwelling in relative obscurity on my Rounder album, *Bluegrass Light*. The others can be heard on the insert record which comes with this book.

Except where noted, these are my own arrangements, and in some cases I've taken liberties with the melodies to suit my style. Even so, they are close enough to the original versions to be easily recognizable. These are all tunes that I particularly like because of their melodic content, chord structure or other more subliminal reasons. I hope you'll enjoy them too.

*Breakfast Special*

# Paddy On The Turnpike

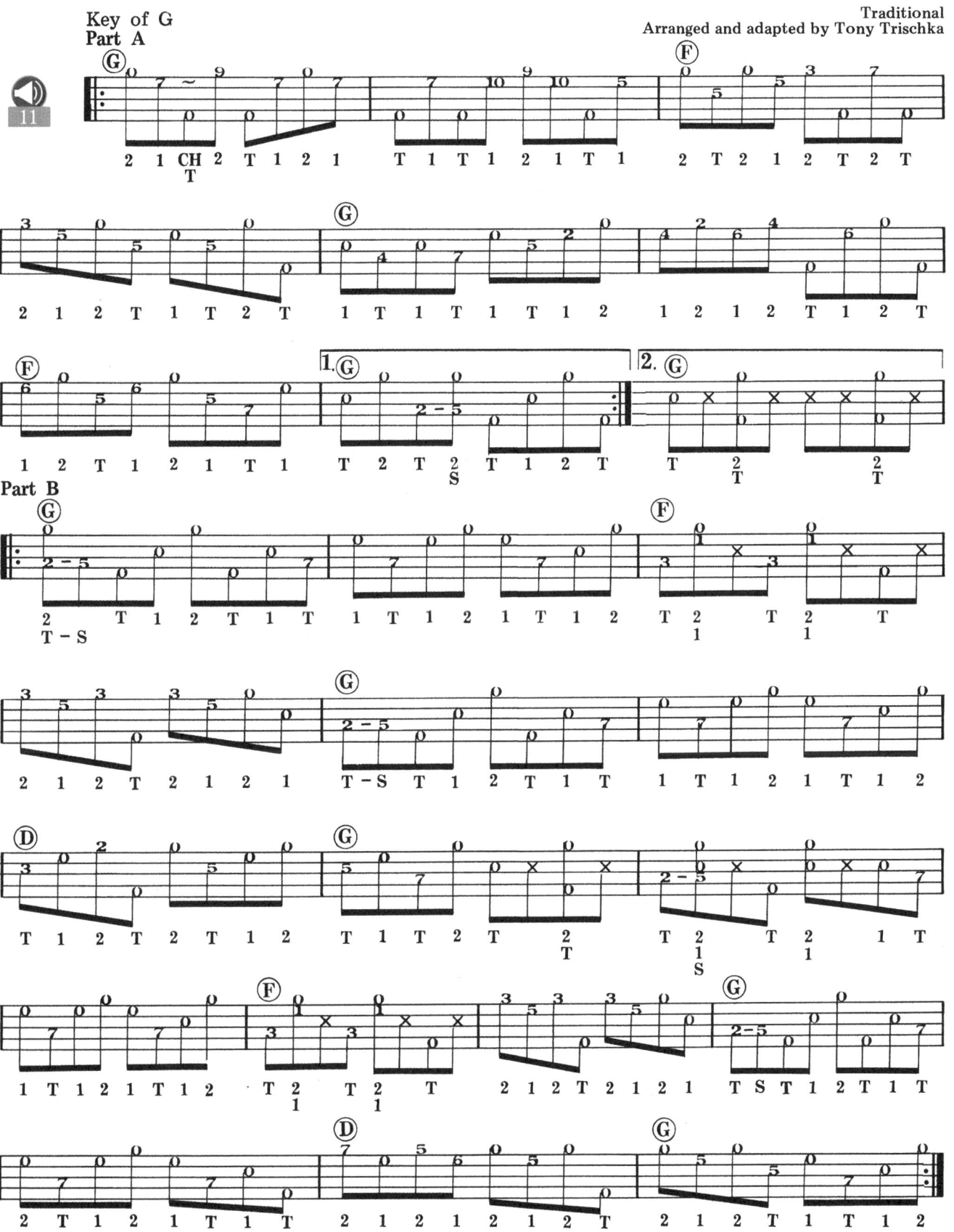

# John Hardy

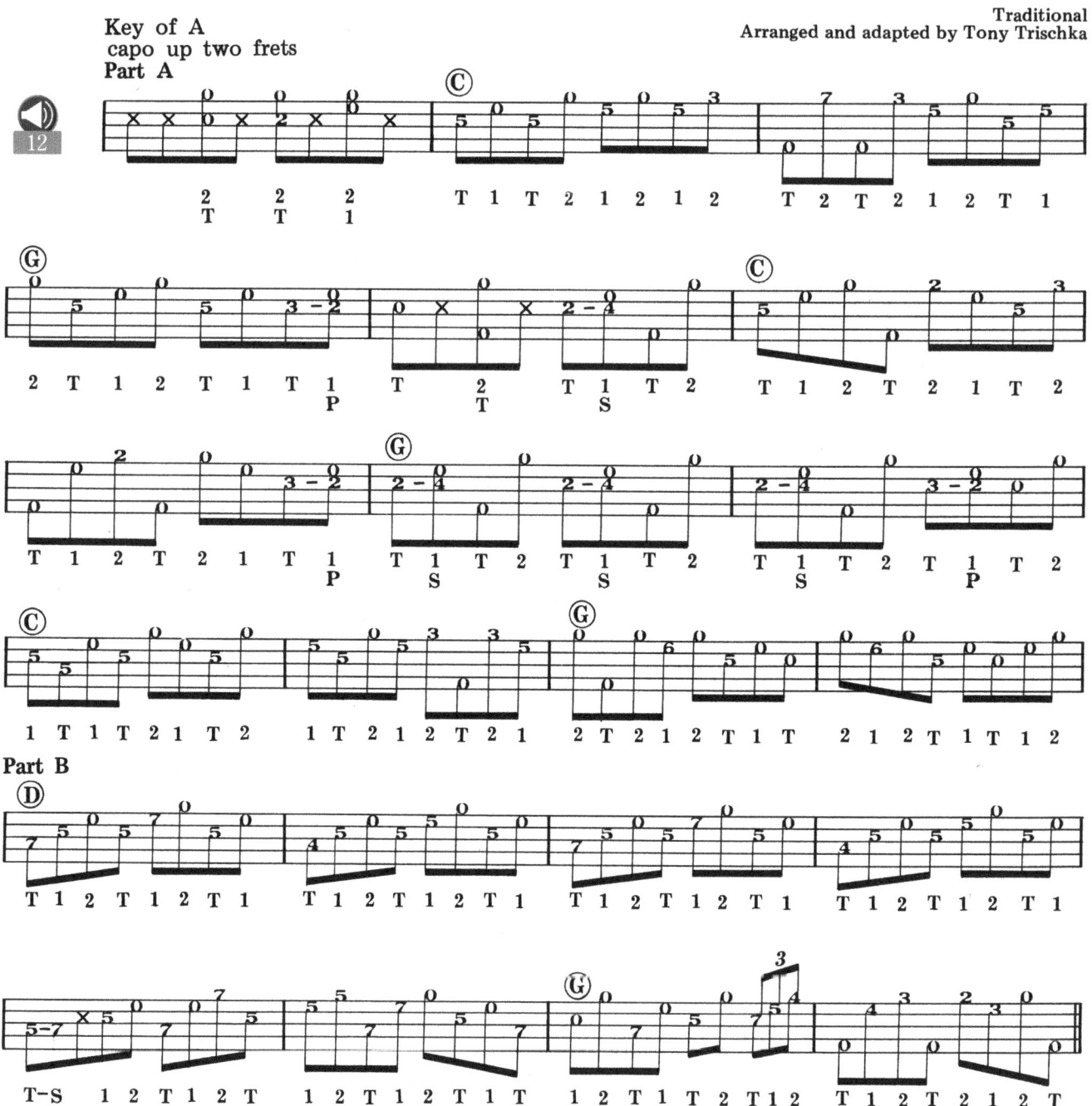

# June Apple

Key of A
capo up two frets

Traditional
Arranged and adapted by Tony Trischka

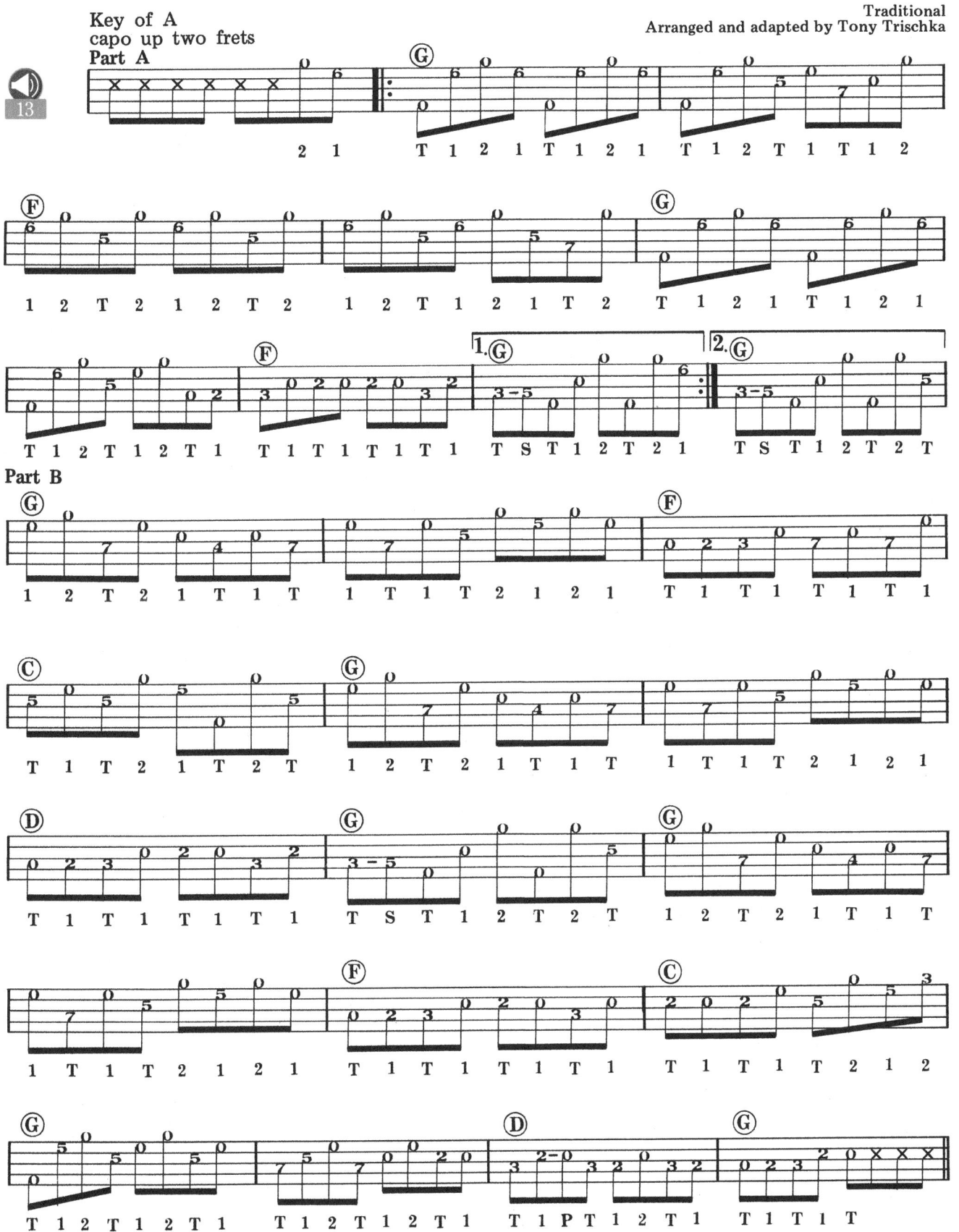

# Rickett's Hornpipe

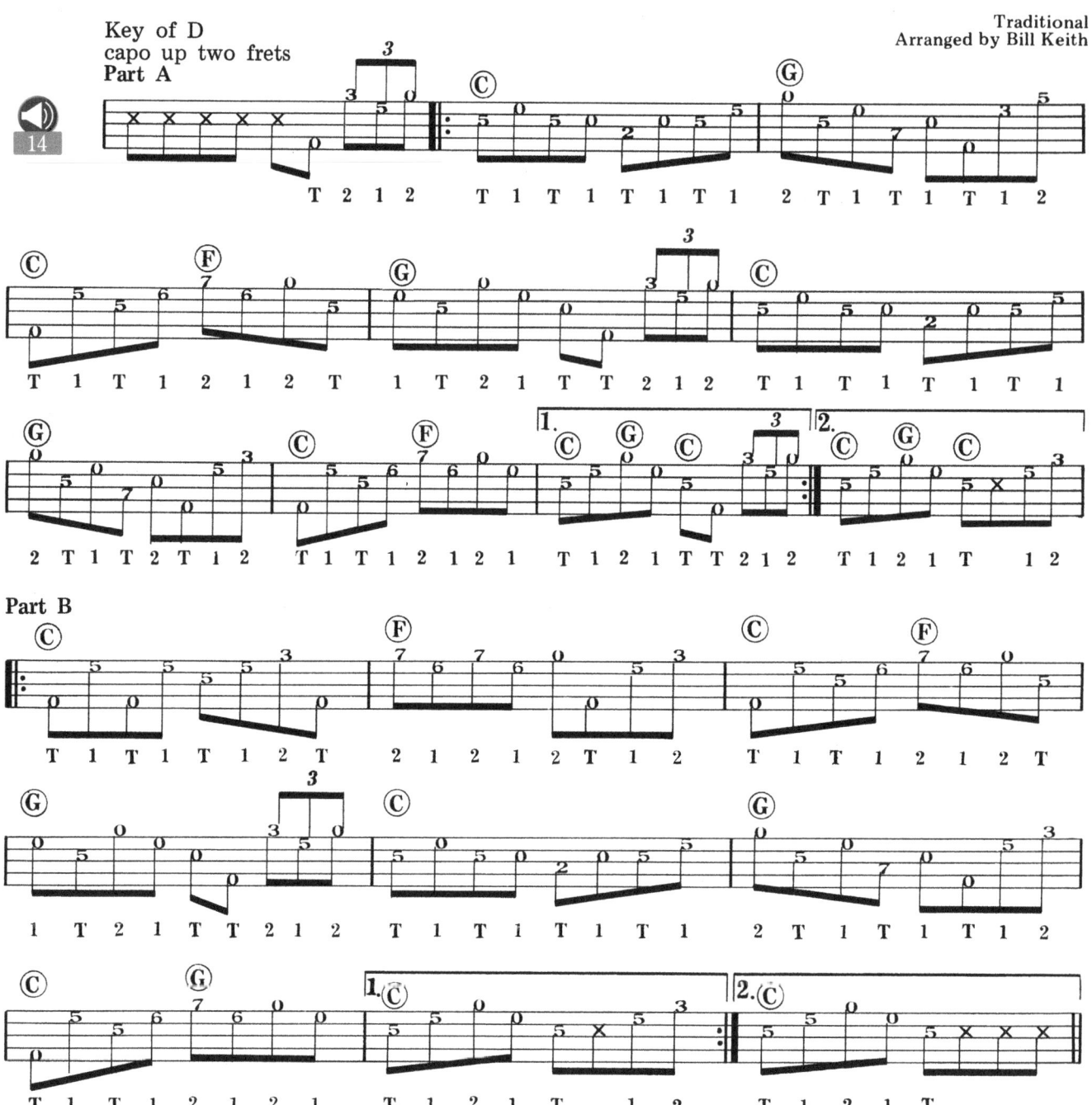

# Soldier's Joy

Traditional
Arranged and adapted by Tony Trischka

Key of D
tuning : GCGBD
capo up two frets

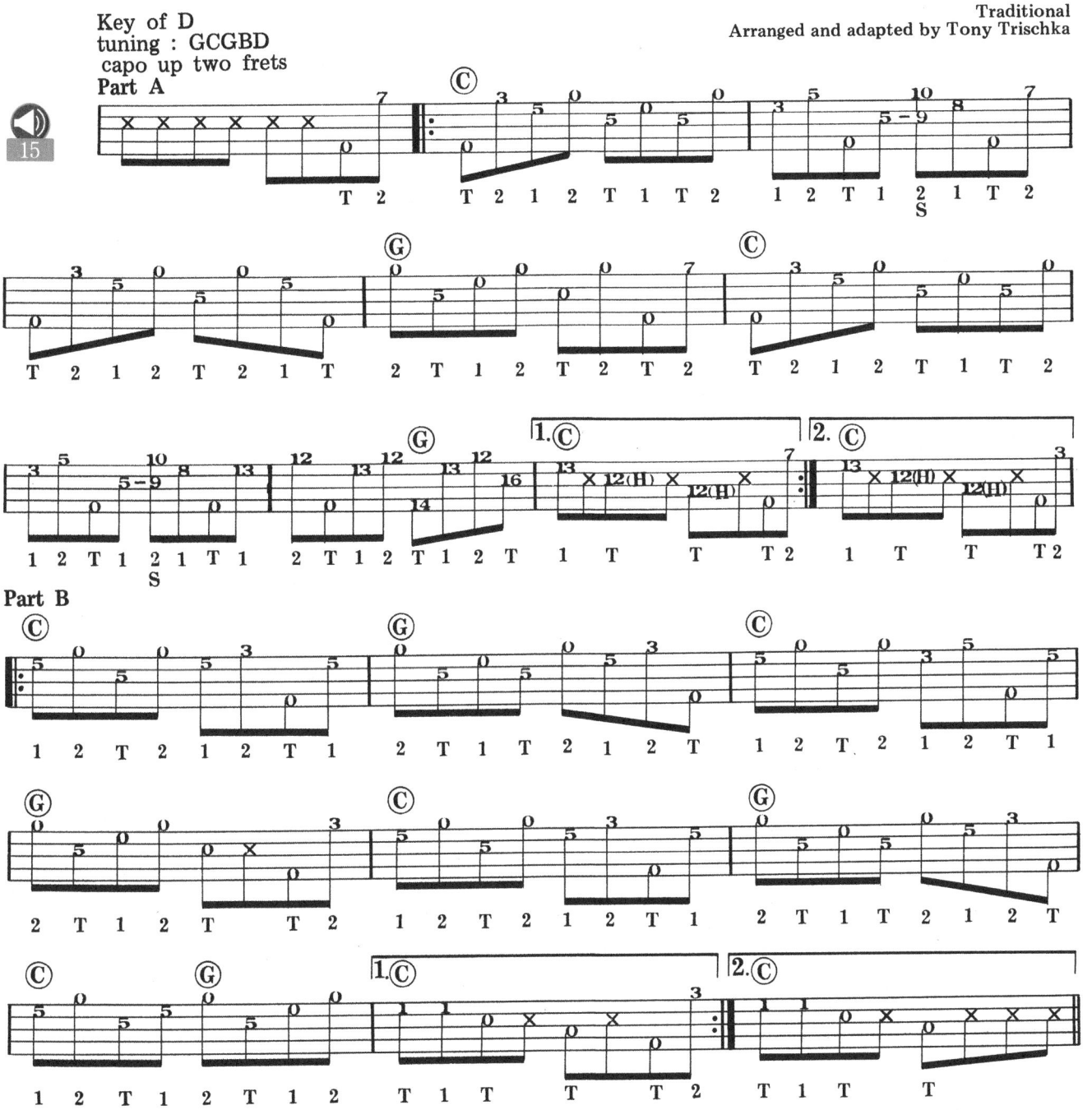

# Red Haired Boy

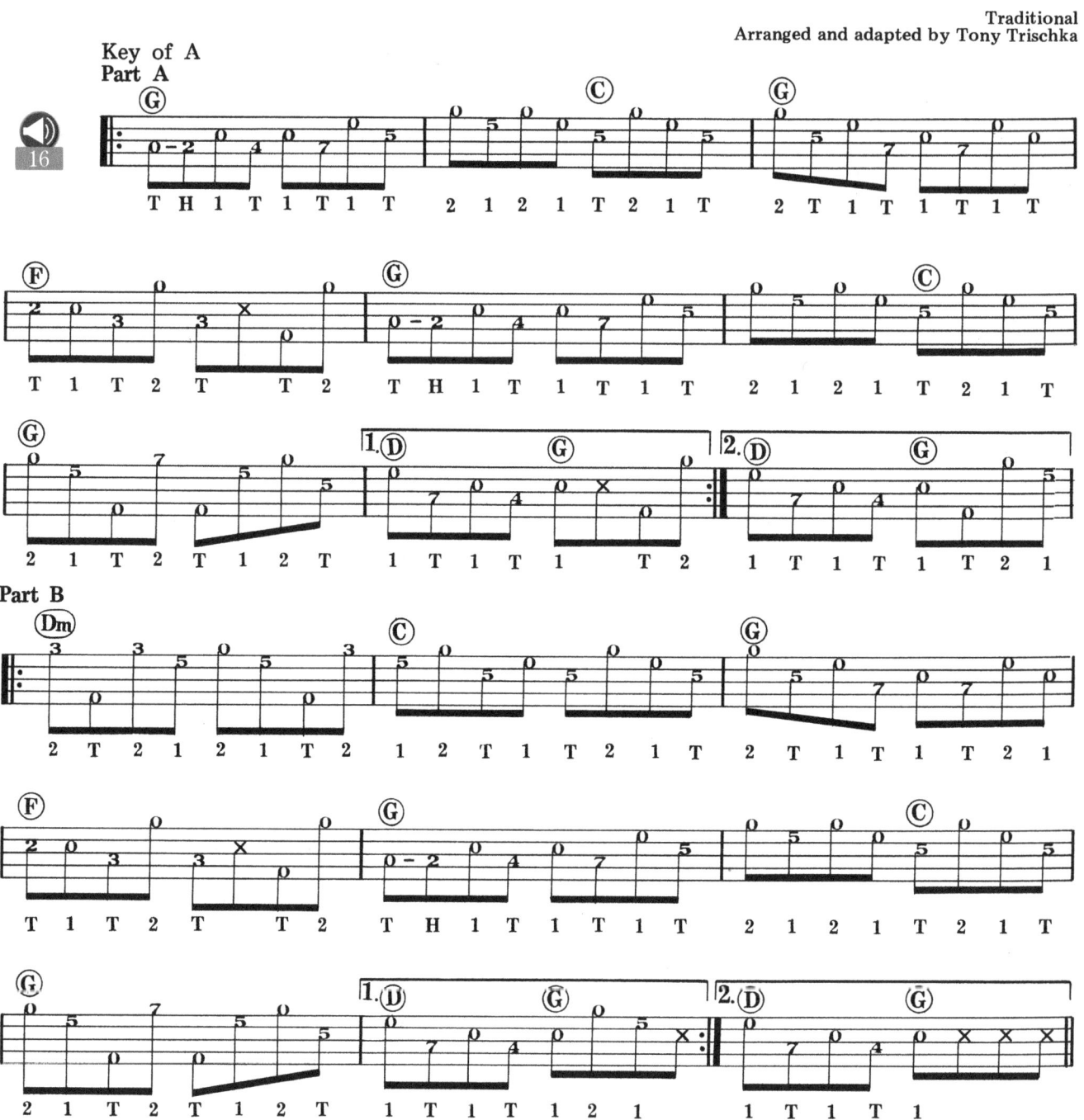

# Sally Goodin

Traditional
Arranged and adapted by Tony Trischka

Key of A
capo up two frets

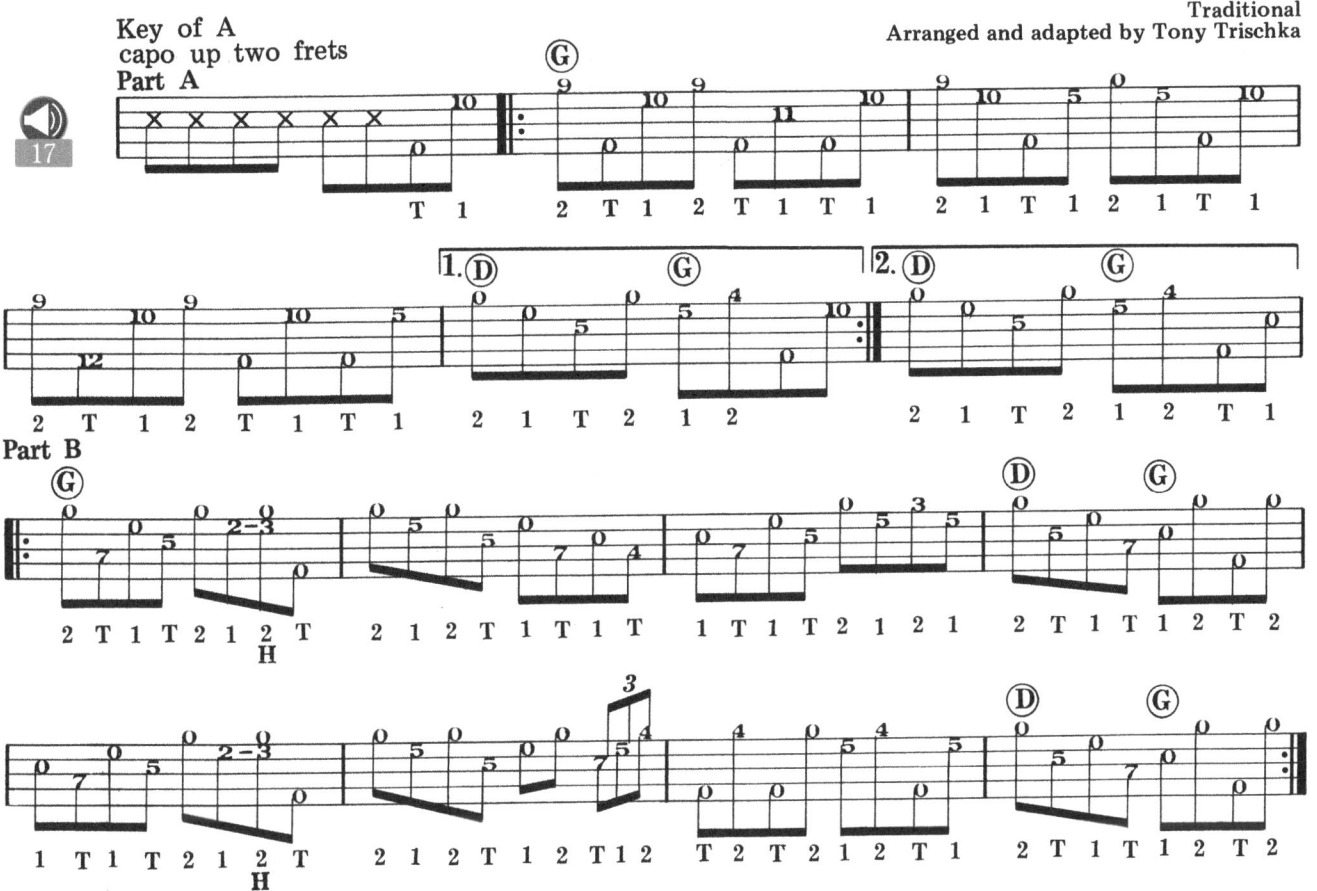

L to R: Jack Hicks, Bill Monroe and Tex Logan

# Fisher's Hornpipe

Traditional
Arranged and adapted by Mark Horowitz

# Sleepy Hollow Real

Key of A
capo up two frets

Part A

Tony Trischka

© 1975 Tony Trischka. All Rights Reserved. Used by Permission.

As played on Tony Trischka's *Bluegrass Light*, Rounder Records 0048

# Twelve Weeks At Sea

© 1975 John Miller. All Rights Reserved. Used by Permission.

As played on Tony Trischka's *Bluegrass Light*, Rounder Records 0048

# Appendices

Music Theory

Although I didn't concentrate too heavily on music theory in the main body of the book, it can really help you to know a few of the basic ideas behind scales and chord structure. Of course, you can play the banjo without any real knowledge of theory (and a lot of people have), but the more you know, the farther you can go in your music.

For starters, you should be aware that there are seven letter names for notes: A, B, C, D, E, F and G. These are called *natural* notes. On a piano keyboard they appear like this:

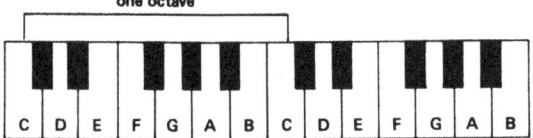

Looking again at the keyboard, the interval between the first A and the second A is called an *octave*. Every octave contains thirteen notes—eight naturals, and five others called flats (♭) or sharps (♯). These are the black keys on the piano. To flat a note you drop down a half step (to the next lower fret on the banjo). To sharp a note you go up a half step. Thus, if your first string open is tuned to D, the first fret will be D♯, the second fret E, and so on for every other string anywhere on the fingerboard.

If you combine the thirteen octave notes consecutively, each a half step apart from the other, you'll have a chromatic scale. Chromatic playing in the melodic style refers to a series of these notes which are put into a particular run or passage.

Out of the thirteen chromatic notes, there are eight which make up the *major* (or do, re, mi) scale. In the key of C, the major scale is C, D, E, F, G, A, B, C. If you look at the piano keyboard you'll notice that there is a whole step (two half steps) between C and D, and between D and E, followed by a half step from E to F, and three more whole steps: F to G, G to A, A to B, concluding with a half step from B to C. This is actually the standard form for any major scale:

whole step, whole step, half step, whole step, whole step, whole step, half step.

Here's a chart, devised by Peter Wernick, that shows you exactly what's going on in each scale.

| | (do) | (re) | (mi) | (fa) | (sol) | (la) | (si) | (do) |
|---|---|---|---|---|---|---|---|---|
| Key | 1 | 2 | 3 | 4 | 5 | 6 | 7 | 8 |
| A | A | B | C♯ | D | E | F♯ | G♯ | A |
| B | B | C♯ | D♯ | E | F♯ | G♯ | A♯ | B |
| C | C | D | E | F | G | A | B | C |
| D | D | E | F♯ | G | A | B | C♯ | D |
| E | E | F♯ | G♯ | A | B | C♯ | D♯ | E |
| F | F | G | A | A♯ | C | D | E | F |
| G | G | A | B | C | D | E | F♯ | G |
| A♯ | A♯ | | | | | | | A♯ |
| C♯ | C♯ | | | | | | | C♯ |
| D♯ | D♯ | | | | | | | D♯ |
| F♯ | F♯ | | | | | | | F♯ |
| G♯ | G♯ | | | | | | | G♯ |

This chart can also help you construct chords. All major chords are made up of the 1, 3 and 5 notes. For example, a basic G chord consists of G, B and D; an A chord of A, C♯ and E. If you want to get a minor chord, take the 1 and 5 note and flat the 3 note a half step. A G minor chord would then be G, B♭, and D; an A minor chord A, C, E. These three-note chords (major or minor) are called *triads*.

Of course, these aren't the only chords floating around. You can add other notes to the basic triads to come up with more colorful chords. For instance, you can get a 6th chord by adding the sixth note of the scale to a triad. This will result in a jazzy sound found a lot in "muzak" and in the more soulful playing of people like Hank Williams. Here are two different inversions of the 6th chord found on the banjo:

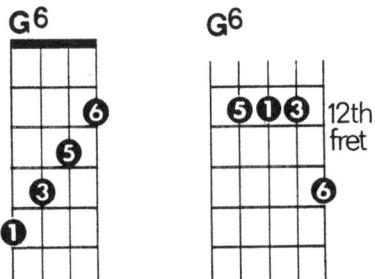

117

If you move the 6 note up a half step you'll get a dominant seventh chord. It's actually the flat of the 7th (or major 7th) chord, but it's more commonly used, especially for leading from a 1 chord to a 4 chord. Here are two inversions of the 7th chord:

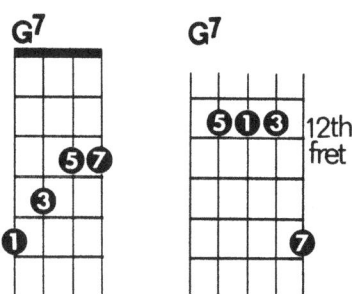

Move the dominant 7th note up one half step and you get a major 7th which gives you a softer jazz feel. Here's a G major 7th.

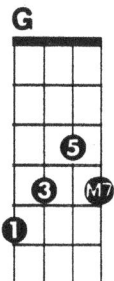

A 9th chord, of course, adds the 9 note, which is the same as the 2 note taken up one octave. A true 9th chord is made up of the 1, 3, 5, 7♭ and 9 notes, but you can leave out one or two of these notes and still have the chord sound like a 9th. Here are two inversions of a G9 chord.

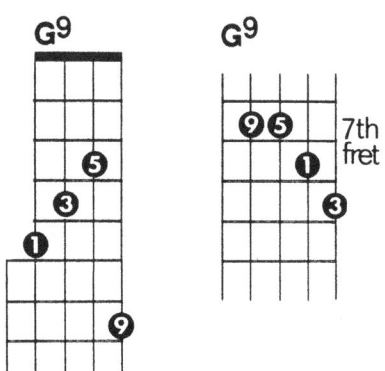

Two final chords I want to talk about are the *augmented* and *diminished*. An augmented chord sharps the fifth degree of the scale a half step (1, 3, 5♯), and can be used for going from a 1 chord to a 4 chord. Try this G augmented:

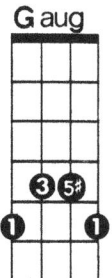

The interesting thing is that this chord repeats every four frets in a different inversion. Thus a G augmented is the same as a B augmented which is the same as a D♯ augmented and so on. Try it for yourself.

A diminished chord flats the 3, 5, and dominant 7th notes a half step. Here's a diminished G:

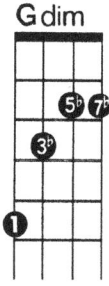

This chord also repeats, this time every three frets.

Although some of these chords are standing on the outskirts of bluegrass, that doesn't mean you shouldn't experiment with them. Naturally a G diminished with an added 9th won't have much of a place in a tune like "Uncle Pen," but you can construct licks out of some of these chords and integrate them into the steady stream of your playing without causing too much consternation. Also, you can use these chords to create your own music which goes beyond the normal boundaries of bluegrass. In short, don't be afraid to experiment.

A Few Notes on Setting Up Your Banjo
to Play Bluegrass
by Tom Hosmer[5]

In this appendix I'm going to take a few things for granted. First, I assume that you already own a bluegrass style banjo. Secondly, I believe that most of you know what I mean by the terms action, frets, nut, neck angle and so on. Thirdly, I take it for granted that all of you are serious enough about bluegrass banjo playing to want to own a first-rate banjo, if not today, then in the future. I hope to be able to explain to you now, in simple English, how to get the most sound and the best feel out of your instrument.

The Frame

By frame I mean a Mastertone style frame. (From here on I will only use the term *Mastertone* to refer to this type of banjo frame.) The basic rule of thumb here is that everything has to be tight. The banjo may be thought of as a machine rather than a musical instrument. To get the best sound there must be no loose parts to interfere with the sustain and the transfer of vibration.

The part of the banjo that will affect the tone more than anything else is the tone ring. It must be made of good quality machined brass; and just as important, it must fit tightly. Many perfectly set up banjos sound dead in the high registers due to an ill-fitting tone ring. Of course, to check on the fit of the tone ring, the banjo frame must be completely disassembled. If the tone ring comes off easily, it is too loose. This problem is especially evident in the winter months when the indoor relative humidity is low. The wood rim shrinks and the tone ring becomes loose. I have seen this problem occur on many new Mastertones. It can be cured by using a Dampit humidifier (lay it along the resonator flange when the banjo is in the case). This is a solution to a problem that should not occur in the first place. Some instruments suffer this problem to such an extent that the rim has to be shimmed and the tone ring refit. Needless to say, if your banjo suffers from this problem, it is best to take it to a qualified repairman who has a reputation for knowing something about banjos.

If your tone ring is tight and the other metal parts seem to be in good condition, the first thing to do is to tighten the head. It has to be extremely tight to give good sound and it may take a couple of days to get it completely tightened. Don't try to go all the way in five minutes or you stand a very good chance of breaking the head, especially if you've just put it on. When you finally get it tight you should not be able to push in the surface of the head more than 1/16 to 1/8 of an inch at its center.

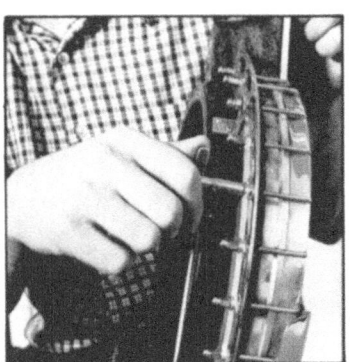

You should have a good tailpiece that will push the strings down toward the head and exert pressure on the bridge. The Waverly tailpiece, which is standard equipment on many modern banjos, is certainly the best and least expensive one on the market. It is very sturdy and the string tension is adjustable. There are many more expensive tailpieces, but there are none that are appreciably better to warrant the extra expense. The tailpiece should be tightened just like a bracket to insure stability.

The Neck

Once you have made sure the frame is in order you must make sure the neck has no problems. The first thing to see to is the place where the neck is attached to the frame. Mastertone-style banjos use a coordinator rod system to both attach the neck and adjust the height of the strings from the fingerboard. The neck must be very tight to the rim and it must fit perfectly. This is usually not a problem with factory made instruments; however, many custom-made necks do not fit their rims with as much precision as could be desired. This affects stability and sound, and if fit is a problem, it should only be solved by a competent repairman. If the neck fits well, it should be secured very tightly with the coordinator rods. (Mastertones made from the forties through the sixties employ only one coordinator rod. The other neck bolt is secured with a nut.) The only rod that is used to adjust the action is the one closest to the resonator. I will explain how to adjust the action with the rod after I cover the other aspects of the neck.

[5]Tom is an excellent instrument repairman from Syracuse, New York. He's also a fine fiddle player as is evidenced by his winning the New York State Fiddle Championship in 1974.

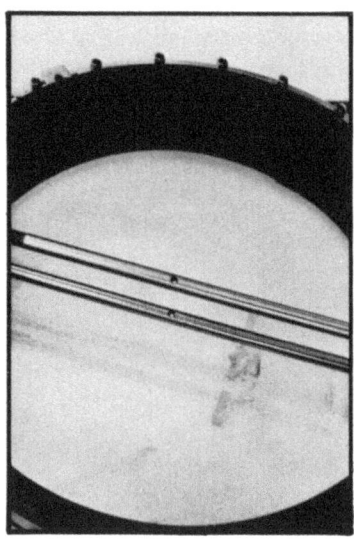

Once the neck is secured to the frame it should be visually inspected for any problems that will effect "playability." It is best that the banjo be strung up at that time. The frets should be high, round and level with respect to one another. If they are grooved, worn, flattened and uneven—which is usually the case in an older banjo—it is best to have this problem attended to before attempting to set up the banjo. Again it is imperative that this work be done by a repairman who knows his trade. I prefer to use Martin-style guitar frets when I refret banjos. They are small enough to give a good feel to the neck, but still large enough to allow dressing and reprofiling as the frets wear. Frets of this size help good sustain and are high enough so that the fingers don't get stuck on the fingerboard.

When the banjo is strung up, the neck should be sighted to see how straight it is. It should not be perfectly straight; there should be a gradual hollow from the first to the seventh fret, and then the board should be level from there on. This allows the action to be uniform from the lower to the higher registers. If the neck is perfectly straight, the action in the high registers must be very high in order for the lower registers to be played without buzzing. A slight relief from frets one through seven allows a lower action in the high registers without sacrificing the punch needed down low. When the banjo neck is refretted, the fingerboard is usually *trued* so that the truss rod (running through the neck) will operate to give the proper relief when adjusted.

The truss rod on most banjos may be adjusted while the banjo is strung up, with a few exceptions —notably the older models of Baldwins and Odes where the truss rod can only be adjusted by removing the neck. With Mastertones, the adjustable end of the truss rod is found underneath the bell-shaped piece of plastic on the headstock. A half turn in either direction will usually correct any problems, but if the rod turns hard or it will not correct the problem, get the instrument to the repairman.

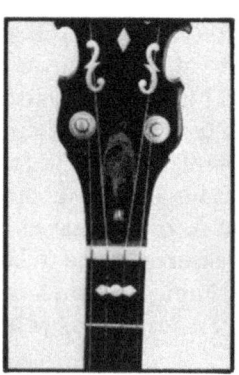

The nut is the next thing to look at. The strings should be just high enough so that they will not buzz on the first fret when the banjo is played *very hard*. Once they are adjusted for height, the nut should be cut down so that the strings are resting on their grooves and not in them. Unless you have the proper saws and files (you guessed it), this job is best left to the repairman.

Now we are ready to adjust the string height. This is a job you can do yourself, but if you're not adept with wrenches and other tools, shag it over to your friendly repairman. The banjo should be strung up and in playing condition. It should have a 5/8" bridge. The resonator should be removed. The neck should be adjusted for the desired degree of straightness with relief. Play the banjo and decide how much higher or lower the action should be and then take the tension off the strings. If you look at the coordinator rod near the tailpiece you will see a nut on either side of the wood rim or, as in the case with Odes and Baldwins, a thumb nut on the inside of the rim and recessed screw on the outside. The procedure is the same for either construction.

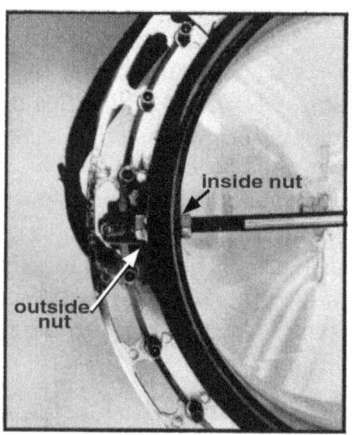

If you wish to lower the action, loosen the inside nut and tighten the outside nut. The coordinator rod may be kept from moving by inserting a nail or awl in the hole that is provided for this purpose in the center of the rod. The action may be raised by reversing the procedure. The neck angle is changed by actually warping the wood rim of the banjo. This allows the neck contact to remain the same. This method, of course, can only account for a small variance in string height. If the neck is put on at the wrong angle, causing the action to be a quarter of an inch too high, the coordinator rod will not correct for this much deviation. Factory-made instruments usually do not suffer from this problem as do hand made banjos that are sometimes the first efforts of an inexperienced craftsman. Banjos of the latter variety can usually be bought at bargain prices, but the saving is usually lost in what it costs to have a good repairman reset the neck. Anyway, back to string height. What's comfortable for one person may be masochistically high for someone else. Try to stay away from really low actions. A low action is great when you are sitting alone playing at moderate volume. However, when you are playing in a band with three or four other instruments and you have to dig in, a low action will just cause a lot of noise. Almost every professional banjo player I know has what I consider to be a high action, and this includes driving players like J. D. Crowe and Bill Emerson. At the higher frets, the action is often about ¼".

Of course, the quality of the banjo can dictate how high the action must be. A pre-war Mastertone that is very loud can be set a little lower since you don't have to play it so hard; but a modern factory-made banjo, like a Fender or Baldwin, or a new Mastertone, will not usually have the punch of the pre-war instruments and will need to be adjusted higher. It may take three or four adjustments of the coordinator rod, tuning and detuning the strings in between, before you get the banjo where you want it. Be patient. After you get your action where it feels good, make sure everything is tight and replace the resonator. You have one more adjustment to make.

### The Bridge

To thin or not to thin—that is the question. It goes without saying that stock banjo bridges are almost all too thick. The amount that you thin your bridge depends on how you play and what kind of sound you want from your banjo. A bridge that is too thin will accentuate the high registers and have a thinner, sharper tone, usually at the expense of the bottom end. By leaving the bridge a little on the thick side, the bottom end will be stronger. You will have to experiment and determine what suits your banjo and your style of playing. Remember not to get the top of the bridge too thin as it will wear out very quickly from the pressure of the strings. The grooves should be just deep enough to keep the string from jumping out, and should be the same size as the string. Don't necessarily depend on the grooves that are put in the bridge at the factory.

The position of the bridge is determined by the harmonic at the twelfth fret. Hit the harmonic on one string and then fret the same string at the twelfth fret. Ideally the two should be in tune with each other to guarantee true fretting in the higher registers. If the fretted note is a little bit sharp on the harmonic, the bridge should be moved a small distance closer to the tailpiece. Reverse this procedure if the fretted note is flat when compared to the harmonic. Keep playing around with the position of the bridge until everything is in tune.

### Fifth String Capo

If you intend to use a capo, you must find a method of raising the fifth string to the required pitch without tuning it up. Enter the fifth string capo. There are two varieties—the kind you screw on to the side of the neck, which I do not recommend, and the use of H. O. railroad spikes, which are hammered into the fingerboard. These I do recommend. Since putting in these spikes requires very small drill bits and some degree of expertise, I do not advise you to do it yourself. Take the banjo to a repairman who definitely knows how to install them. They should be placed at the seventh and ninth frets so that you can play easily in the keys of A and B.

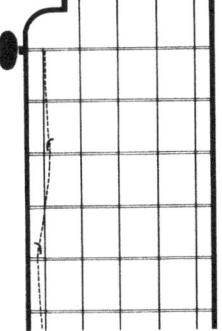

Although I don't recommend fifth string capos that screw on to the side of the neck, there is one that is quite superlative called the *Shubb* capo. It is machined metal and it works very well, as opposed to other brands which operate with a piece of spring wire whose sole purpose seems to be to scrape the finish off the neck and make the fifth string sound like a sitar. They do have their advantages, though, in that you can capo your fifth string anywhere within a six or seven note range with the flick of a finger. So the choice is up to you.

Geared Fifth String Peg

This is an indispensable item for anyone interested in precision tuning (which all of you should be). Prior to the invention of the geared fifth, fifth string pegs had only a 1:1 gear ratio. In other words, you would raise or lower the pitch of the string in direct proportion to the amount you turned the peg. As a result, you would usually over- or undershoot the desired note on your first few tries. Today, however, we are blessed with the geared fifth string peg, which allows for a much finer tuning accuracy. At the moment, there are two recommended brands on the market: Kroll (selling for about $15), and Stewart-MacDonald (selling for about $10). The Kroll peg has a 9:1 gear ratio—for every nine turns of the button there is one revolution of the shaft through which the string goes. The Stewart-MacDonald peg features a 4:1 gear ratio and differs from the Kroll in that it is a straight through peg, thus eliminating the shaft. Either type will do the job, so if you don't already have one, you should pick one up.

Well, that's about it, folks. My only other suggestion is to make sure that the banjo receives proper humidification during the dry months, and to keep both the metal and the wooden parts of the banjo clean; and for Christmas' sake, don't drop it on the floor and break the neck.

Banjo Playing:
Reno-Thompson-Scruggs-Keith Style and Beyond
by Steve Arkin[6]

When you think about it, there is nothing really ingenious or surprising about using a lead instrument like the five-string banjo to play melody. What is far more curious is the fact that the banjo passed through two decades of bluegrass history, during which none of its leading exponents had a fully satisfactory style for even the simplest melodic passage. It is a tribute to Earl Scruggs and his complex and subtle style that the banjo was able to assume such a pre-eminent position in the bluegrass arsenal without being able to fulfill the first requisite of a lead instrument—the ability to execute scales.

All this has changed. A walk through a festival parking lot will quickly inundate the hapless listener with more scales than a 1,000 pound tuna. Major scales, minor scales, chromatic scales, modal scales —ad infinitum/ad nauseum. The age of melodic banjo playing is surely upon us, and it has brought with it a whole new generation of stars who play in this style: Bill Keith, Bobby Thompson, Jack Hicks, Carl Jackson, Larry McNeely, Tony Trischka, Pat Cloud, Courtney Johnson, Alan Munde, etc.

In discussing these new stars, as in discussing their predecessors, one pointless dispute persists in conversations among bluegrass musicians and fans: who should be credited with the development of a particular style? Surely we have all heard that Snuffy Jenkins did it all before Earl Scruggs. Even some of Scruggs' defenders will credit him only with the dissemination of the style, not its creation. It seems to me that anyone listening to these two musicians would realize that Earl's playing is a quantum jump ahead of Snuffy's—much as the latter represents an advance over that early three-finger pioneer, Charlie Poole.

Likewise, there has been much speculation as to whether Don Reno preceded Earl Scruggs in the development of the three-finger bluegrass banjo style, and whether it wasn't just an accident that the style wasn't called "Reno style." Again, this strikes me as an inane argument. Obviously both of these

[6]Reprinted with permission of *Pickin'* Magazine, © 1974.

fine musicians were influenced by Snuffy Jenkins, but it is also obvious to anyone who has heard records of the early Reno that he didn't play like Scruggs then any more than now. Earl's right hand is smoother, more articulate, and more syncopated; his style is tighter and more coherent than Don's. Of course, Don Reno compensates for this with a dazzling, unique, and inventive style of his own. But that's not the point—it is his own, not the progenitor of Scruggs'.

This leads us to look at what I believe to be yet another example of this type of inane argument: whether Bill Keith or Bobby Thompson was the originator of the melodic style. Each claims to have developed this style independently. Thompson dates his innovation to the late 1950's. Keith learned "Devil's Dream" in 1961. From my own vantage point, I'm inclined to believe the genesis was independent. In fact, I was responsible for introducing the two to each other.

I first met Bill Keith in the summer of 1961. At that time, the thing which most impressed me about his playing was the incredible fidelity with which he could duplicate Scruggs' playing—right down to that indescribable tone that has eluded everyone I've ever heard.

Another important aspect was one of the tunes in Keith's repertoire: "Noah's Breakdown." It was not until after I learned Keith's arrangement that I appreciated its true significance. This tune (recorded by Noah Crase in the fifties) had a bridge utilizing the position which would be considered the key to the new style: the alternation between open strings and fretting at the fifth and seventh frets. Runs using this same position were redistributed throughout Keith's playing and had already been dubbed "Keith runs" by his fans.

A third impressive component of his playing back then was the prevalence of Don Stover/Allen Shelton-style syncopation—a rarity in the North, except in that the Shelton "bounce" was advocated by Roger Sprung (by precept and not example).

At this time, the above elements of Keith's playing made a greater impression on me than two newly learned tunes, which were his earliest totally melodic pieces—"Devil's Dream" and "Sailor's Hornpipe." Up to that point neither tune was an established standard in the bluegrass repertoire, though both were very nice fiddle tunes nevertheless. Keith's inspiration to work out these tunes had been suggested by the similarity of the fret positions to "Noah's Breakdown." The term "Keith style" was first applied to his rendition of these tunes.

Over the next two years, Keith's playing improved considerably as his experience spanned long hitches with Jim Rooney, Red Allen, Frank Wakefield, and —most especially—Bill Monroe. Keith's stint with Monroe put the final imprimateur on the new style, although not without input from the Great Man. For one thing, Monroe persistently suggested that Keith avoid entire breaks in the melodic style and frowned on whimsical non sequiturs, such as Keith's introduction of a quotation from "Nola" into "Footprints in the Snow." (Keith got his revenge by recording "Footprints," "Nola" and all, on the recent Warner Brothers' *Muleskinner* album.) By the end of his tenure with Monroe, Keith was the "complete" banjo player—tasteful, flashy, flawless, complex, versatile, and very original.

As with other bluegrass banjo players worth their salt, Keith collected mountains of banjo "trivia"— unusual tunes that require lots of technique and that were difficult to integrate into the bluegrass repertoire. Keith's collection ranged from Bach sonatas to "Mr. Sandman" to an abbreviated (two part) version of "Nola." It was this repertoire which was really the laboratory for new techniques and which ultimately seems to have seduced Keith away from bluegrass altogether and toward the pedal steel—a laboratory instrument if ever there was one.

Shortly after Keith left the *Bluegrass Boys*, he suggested to me that I might profit by the same experience. I was in college at the time, and the prospect of such an exotic summer job was irresistible. Consequently, as soon as my 1964 vacation began, I was on a bus for Nashville and an audition. Bill Monroe was pleased to acquire another, albeit more limited, exponent of the melodic style. I had my summer job.

It was in the course of my travels with Bill that I first met Bobby Thompson. We were backstage in a high school somewhere in the wilds of Georgia and this very martial looking guy with a brush cut came in looking for Bill. After Bill and the stranger exchanged warm greetings, Bill turned to me and asked me to play "something fancy." I think I played "Turkey in the Straw," "Salt Creek," and my own rip-off rendition of "Nola."

At Bill's suggestion, I then surrendered my instrument to the visitor, whom I took to be a "hughlie" (pronounced *hyooglee*—Bill's word for people who come backstage to demonstrate a groundless familiarity with bluegrass stars and to finger their instruments, etc.—i.e., a bluegrass groupie). He wasn't. He was Bobby Thompson, newly returned from the service and "out-of-practice." But not really. He was fantastic: effortless guitar-style, single-string work, dazzling Chet Atkins show-pieces like "Swanee River" and the "Humoresque," simultaneously and (wonder of wonders) melodic banjo playing! I vividly recall a nice rendition of "The Arkansas Traveler" in open D, and "Sugarfoot Rag." All very like—and yet unlike—Keith. And had he heard of Keith? "Yes." Heard him? "No." How then did Thompson, living in the relatively isolated town of Converse, S. C., acquire this "new" style? By his own account, he'd been playing like that for years! Jeepers!

I made sure that I got Bobby's address. When I returned to New York at the end of the summer Keith immediately called me to find out how things had gone with Bill. In the course of the conversation, I mentioned that I had met Bobby Thompson, the best banjo player I had ever heard (although I'm not sure I meant that with utter conviction). There was a long thoughtful silence at the other end of the line —followed by, "Well let's go down and see him." And within an hour I, who earlier that day had emerged from a grueling twenty-three hour bus ride from Nashville, found myself in Keith's car—once again heading south.

We arrived in Converse to find Bobby relaxing on his front porch. He had no advance warning of our arrival, but he greeted us hospitably all the same. He didn't go out of his way to express any emotion upon being introduced to Keith (about whom I am convinced he had heard more than he let on). We were invited inside, and after some idle chatter there commenced a classic Alphonse and Gaston routine: "You play first, Bobby."—"Why don't you kick it off, Bill?" After far too much of this, Bobby picked up his banjo and Bill switched on the tape recorder. But for this important debut, Bobby selected nothing more spectacular than a super-straight Scruggs-style rendition of "Shuckin' the Corn." Keith glowered at me and I could detect him silently questioning whether a two-month diet of grits hadn't eroded my connoisseurship.

After "Shuckin' the Corn" the ball was on Bill's side of the net, and he ran through much of his repertoire of fiddle tunes—finishing up with the abbreviated version of "Nola" which I had learned from him. With that, Bobby announced that he had liked the tune when I had played it for him two months earlier and had, therefore, gone out and bought the sheet music to learn it. He then proceeded to play the entire four parts, and all very, very fancy. Bill's jaw and mine dropped and remained in that position as Bobby winged through all of the flashy stuff he had played for me, plus a few surprises like Duke Ellington's "Caravan." As before, my dominant emotion was serendipity: that such a fine musician could have remained so obscure—just a footnote on some old Carl Story and *Jim and Jesse* records.

Keith's reaction was more constructive. He retired to Boston with the precious tape of that encounter to emerge, some months later, with virtually all of it assimilated into his repertoire. At that point, it would be fair to say that Bobby was an influence on Bill. And yet, the tunes Bill learned from him were fully incorporated into Keith's richer, if less flashy style.

Even with much of Bobby's repertoire under his belt, Keith's playing remained uniquely his own. Bobby Thompson plays with the effortless ease of the studio musician: infinite versatility, first in one style, then the other—melodic, Scruggs, single-string. Bill Keith's playing is more integrated, more architectural, more homogenized. His melodic passages merge imperceptibly with his rhythmically and harmonically complex Scruggs style. Single-string is a last resort for him. His playing throughout is dominated by a sophisticated chord structure—a legacy from his early years as a tenor banjo player in Brockton, Mass.

It is ironic that, although Keith was for years the better known exponent of the style, most of the melodic players he influenced utilize the melodic technique in a manner that more closely resembles Thompson's playing. I think the main reason for this is that Keith's style is just too complex and difficult for most newcomers to want to sink their teeth into. It requires a grasp of Scruggs-style basics and chord theory that are a chore to learn for a new picker wanting to get right down to the latest hot licks.

And yet perhaps it is as misleading to talk of melodic-style banjo playing as it would be to speak of melodic-style trumpet playing. Now that the capacity for melodic banjo playing has been established, any number of individual styles are possible—each having perhaps as little to do with the other as Miles Davis has to do with Henry James. The experimentation has now gone even further, however, with some banjo players exploring the "chromatic" style briefly mentioned at the beginning of the article. The melodic style uses only the notes of the familiar major and minor (diatonic) scale. True chromatic playing utilizes all twelve notes of the chromatic scale and is characterized by nonharmonic tones and dissonant notes. It offers complete freedom to the banjo player. Pat Cloud, Tony Trischka and Peter

Schwimmer are three good examples of such musicians in the vanguard of this experimentation.

The floodgates were opened, and suddenly, no note was too weird, no chord too far out, no passage too difficult. Chords which had previously been at home only in jazz—major sevenths, thirteenths, aug-minished's, demented's—now found themselves coexisting congruously with centuries-old fiddle tunes. The myth that the banjo is a limited instrument rapidly faded and, as it faded, one fine banjo player after another slipped outside the world of bluegrass and into the larger community of just-plain musicians.

While I find it delightful that such a vast range of possibilities is now before us, I think that all lovers of bluegrass music are saddened to see so many of the most outstanding musicians defect to other musical idioms. The best hope of keeping them at home where they belong, is for the dyed-in-the-wool traditionalists to allow the experimenters to coexist peacefully with the high lonesome sound we all know and love. If bluegrass music can become as rich and diverse as its potential, we might even see the day when Bill Keith is seduced back from his apostacy on the pedal steel.

Vic Jordan backstage at the Grand Ole Opry

# Discography

If you're not living near a well-stocked record store, you may find some of these records (the ones that aren't on a major label) hard to find. If this is the case, your best bet is to order from one of these two mail order companies:

The Rounder Records
186 Willow Avenue
Somerville, Massachusetts, 02144

County Sales
Department T
Box 191
Floyd, Virginia 24091

They both carry an excellent supply of easy-and hard-to-find records in the bluegrass and country vein. In addition, they release their own albums which are known for their integrity of content and high quality graphics and recording.

This discography does not include those records which are already listed with the tablature. Also, you should keep in mind that this list is only current as of 1975. In the years ahead there will be many more albums to add. To keep up with the latest releases you should check the record review sections of *Bluegrass Unlimited* (Box 111, Broad Run, Virginia 22014), *Frets* 20605 Lazaneo, Cupertino, Ca. 95014.

In addition, there's one other magazine which should be of particular interest to you. This is *The Banjo Newsletter* (1310 Hawkins Lane, Annapolis, Maryland 21401). It comes out once a month and contains tablature and interviews with banjoists in both the bluegrass and old timey fields. I highly recommend this!

| | |
|---|---|
| **Ben Eldridge:** | Mike Auldridge's two albums (Takoma D-1033, D-1041) and any of the Seldom Scene's Records (Rebel) |
| **Jack Hicks:** | Bill Monroe *Bean Blossom* (MCA 2-9002), *Kenny Baker Country* (County 736), Buck White and the Down Home Folks *In Person* (County 760) |
| **Carl Jackson:** | *Banjo Player* (Capitol ST-11166) |
| **Vic Jordan:** | *The Jim and Jesse Show* (Prize PRS-49804), *Banjo Nashville* (Sugar Hill SH-3704) |
| **Bill Keith:** | *Strictly Clean and Decent* (Rounder 0084), *The David Grisman Rounder Album* (Rounder 0069), *Muleskinner* (Ridge Runner RR 106) |
| **Alan Munde:** | *Banjo Sandwich* (Ridge Runner RRR 0001), *Sam and Alan* (Ridge Runner RRR 0007) |
| **Bobby Thompson:** | Bill Monroe *Uncle Pen* (MCA Records) |
| **Eric Weissberg:** | Deliverance *Rural Free Delivery* (Warner Brothers BS 2720) |
| **Tony Trischka:** | *Heartlands* (Rounder 0062), *Banjoland* (Rounder 0087) |
| **Peter Wernick:** | *Dr. Banjo Steps Out* (Flying Fish FF 046), *Hot Rize* (Flying Fish FF 206) |

The following records feature a few other fine melodic pickers who are not discussed in this book.

| | |
|---|---|
| **Jimmy Arnold:** | *Strictly Arnold* (Rebel SLP-1538) |
| **Bob Black:** | *Ladies on the Steamboat* (Ridge Runner RRR 018) |
| **Bela Fleck:** | *Across the Tracks* (Rounder Records) |
| **Dave Griffiths:** | *Workingman's Banjo* (BMA #138) |
| **John Hickman:** | *Don't Mean Maybe* (Rounder 0101) |
| **Bill Knopf:** | *San Andreas Quickstep* (Ridge Runner RRR 020) |
| **Larry McNeely:** | *Rhapsody for Banjo* (Flying Fish FF 025) |
| **Butch Robins:** | *Fragments of My Imagination* (Rounder 0104) |
| **Garland Shuping:** | *On Banjo* (Old Homestead 90038) |

# Song Index

| | | | |
|---|---|---|---|
| 54 | Are You Missing Me | 93 | Jordan's Hornpipe |
| 36 | Arkansas Traveler | 109 | June Apple |
| 84 | Bill Cheatham | 53 | Katy Hill |
| 34 | Blackberry Blossom | 35 | Little Sadie |
| 88 | Cold Sailor | 98 | Lonesome Blues |
| 21 | Cripple Creek | 89 | Lonesome Fiddle Blues |
| 76 | Cross Country | 75 | Muddy Water |
| 56 | Devil Dance | 38 | New Camptown Races |
| 66 | Devil's Dream | 22 | Old Joe Clark |
| 85 | Done Gone | 40 | Opus 57 In G Minor |
| 97 | Dusty Miller | 107 | Paddy On The Turnpike |
| 67 | Eighth Of January | 112 | Red Haired Boy |
| 68 | Fire On The Mountain | 110 | Rickett's Hornpipe |
| 114 | Fisher's Hornpipe | 113 | Sally Goodin |
| 57 | Foxfire | 69 | Shuckin' The Corn |
| 75 | Gardens And Memories | 115 | Sleepy Hollow Real |
| 80 | Grey Eagle | 111 | Soldier's Joy |
| 79 | Indian Blood | 92 | Turkey In The Straw |
| 108 | John Hardy | 116 | Twelve Weeks At Sea |